The
Cycling Adventures
of Coconut Head

The Cycling Adventures of Coconut Head

A North American Odyssey

TED SCHREDD

Whitecap Books
Vancouver / Toronto

The information in this book is true and complete to the best of our
knowledge. All recommendations are made without guarantee on the part
of the author or Whitecap Books Ltd. The author and publisher disclaim
any liability in connection with the use of this information. For additional
information please contact Whitecap Books Ltd., 351 Lynn Avenue,
North Vancouver, BC V7J 2C4.

Edited by Carolyn Bateman
Cover design by Rose Cowles
Interior design by Rose Cowles
Cover photograph by Aleck MacKinnon

Printed and bound in Canada by D.W. Friesen and Sons Ltd.,
Altona, Manitoba.

Canadian Cataloguing in Publication Data

Schredd, Ted.
The cycling adventures of Coconut Head

ISBN 1-55110-398-2

1. Schredd, Ted—Journeys—United States. 2. Bicycle touring—
United States. 3. United States—Description and travel. 4.
Bicycle touring—Canada. I. Title.
GV1051.S37A3 1996   796.640973   C95-911137-9

The publisher acknowledges the assistance of the Canada Council
and the Cultural Services Branch of the Government of British Columbia
in making this publication possible.

This book
is dedicated
to my fabulous wife Deanna
in hope that we can spend more time together
playing on this wonderful planet.
It is also dedicated to all
the dreamers of the world
whether they know
they are dreamers yet
or not.

Contents

Read
all this stuff
before you read
the other stuff

The Cycling Adventures of Coconut Head is about how my life took a quantum leap by following my heart. That leap took place while I rode my bicycle around North America.

On October 4, 1992, I left on an 8,000-mile cycling adventure to promote cycling and alternate forms of transportation. My plan was to start in Vancouver, B.C., head south to San Diego, travel east towards Texas, on to the tip of Florida, then up the east coast into Canada and finish in Ottawa. During the ten months of the trip, my partner and I experienced astronomical physical, mental, and spiritual challenges.

I was born and raised as the last child of six in Edmonton, Alberta. I moved away when I was twenty to pursue a career as a professional ski bum. Working and skiing in Lake Louise, Alberta, really opened my eyes to a world of different culture and to traveling. So many Australians, for example, had left their home thousands of miles away to be dishwashers and to ski the winters away. Where I grew up nobody traveled—they just bought houses and got jobs. This was the birth of the travel seed within me.

I moved to Vancouver, B.C., in 1989. From there I continued to be a ski bum, but I also tried sandwich making, cellular phone sales, and one of my all-time favorite jobs, teaching fancy Frisbee moves to schoolkids. I lived in a small apartment and had managed to accumulate thousands of dollars of frivolous credit card debt. My life had no real meaning. I wanted to travel, to meet people, experience new things. I wanted to see if there was more to life than just existing.

In the last week of August 1992 a friend of mine came over to tell me he had sold all his stuff and was moving to Alaska. Now that sounded like fun! I wished him well and visions of travel plums danced in my head. In less than fifteen minutes I had decided I too was going on an adventure.

Where should I go? Palm trees fascinated me and so did Florida; I could ride my bike to Florida and then back up the east coast to Ottawa! In the early part of the twentieth century a man traveled around the world in eighty days with only eighty dollars. If he could do that, I certainly could do this trip on a bicycle.

I could get exercise and fresh air, it would be inexpensive, and I could do my part to heal the earth. Besides, plane rides cost too much and I wanted others to see the benefit of a bicycle. Since the whole idea was kind of outrageous, I figured I could get some media attention along the way and spread the good word about riding a bike.

A few months before I left, I met an environmentalist who said, "We pollute too much, save the planet!" This same earth lover drove a 427 Corvette that got six miles to the gallon. This sort of environmentalism frustrates the hell out of me. The only way to change people is to lead them by example. You can't tell people to *do* anything.

I had no experience in bike touring, and an old bike with bald tires, but I had a mission. "EnviroRide: To encourage people to put less pollution into the air."

My riding partner would be Lisa Steinbeck. She was sweet and beautiful, with long hair and a huge heart. She was born in Calgary and had backpacked extensively through Europe. We had met only a month before on the patio deck of a restaurant. I immediately asked her to come on the trip with me. She said yes and we both gave away all of our worldly possessions and moved out of our apartments. We lived in a friend's closet to save money and get to know each other a little better.

This would be the first bike trip for both of us. Both Lisa and I were average people. We did absolutely no training or special preparations for EnviroRide. I figured we could "fake it till we make it."

For four weeks I tried to get some support in the form of a sponsorship. The only thing I did get was a lot of no's. No money, no equipment, no nothing. Stephen, a friend of mine I had met in Vancouver, was a holistic doctor and gave me numerous contacts around the country for possible accommodation along the way. These contacts were all personal friends or business associates of his.

With only three days left before our planned departure date, I received a letter from my Gramma Schredd who lives on the great Canadian prairies.

Gramma was a very inspirational person in my life. At ninety-three years old Gramma stayed healthy taking care of her massive vegetable garden all summer long just as she had been doing every year for the past sixty-nine years. Besides her enthusiasm about life she had always been incredibly generous. I thought she was sending me a financial donation but it was only a letter that read:

Dear Ted,

I am very excited about your biking adventure and wanted to share some Schredd family wisdom with you. This philosophy has been invaluable to the level of health and happiness in my life. Please consider it before you step into your new unknown world.

My Gramma Schredd told me this in the summer of 1921 when I was about to leave Germany to live in Canada with my husband, your Grampa, after the Great War. Sure things were different. Kids had to walk miles just to get bratwurst, but I think the philosophy is the same.

My Gramma Schredd told me, "You see, Greta, even though you may think you have no control over your life you actually do. Even though everybody around you may say that you had good luck, or bad luck, there is no such thing as luck."

I believe you pick up feelings from others as well as communicating your feelings to the people around you. If everyone around you is sad, chances are you are going to be sad. If everyone around you is scared, you'll probably be scared. If everybody around you is happy and smiling, having a nice time, you probably will too.

Have you ever heard that little voice in your head that says, "You're just not good enough." You're not good enough for that pretty boy or girl, for your family, you're not good enough to have the things you want, you're not good enough for marriage, you're not good enough to accomplish your dreams."

Or maybe you've heard the little voice say, "This isn't it. She's not it, he's not it, this town's not it, this meal's not it, this new shirt is not it." You can make yourself so angry trying to change things that have already happened.

That little voice is also saying, "Something's wrong! Something's wrong with my hair, my face, my clothes, my dog, my spouse, my life." How is it possible to be happy if there's always something wrong?

That little voice, it's not you! It never was you, it never will be you. Let's call the little voice, "mind poo."

I saw you come onto this planet as a beautiful baby, full of love, awe, and wonderment. As you grew older you learned to accept the mind poo as a part of your self. But you have a choice. You don't have to listen to that voice . . . you can listen to your heart.

When you listen to your heart you meet the right people at the right time and you follow your hunches. Everything that happens to you is the best you could have ever imagined. I am sure you have experienced moments like this throughout your life. In this state you feel great power, as if the whole world wants to help you. Great Gramma Schredd called this feeling the state of Spirit.

Why would Ted, I mean the real Ted, ever want to harm or tell yourself that you were just not good enough?

Inside every human being is a secret knowledge that can guide you to wherever you want to go. You can deny it or you can try it. Ted, if you trust that everything will be OK, people will take care of you. Or you can listen to mind poo!

All of our lives we were taught that the mind poo was a part of us, that everything just happens by chance, but inside every human being is a superstar. The secret to life is to control your destiny and let that superstar shine. So avoid that mind poo, trust that everything will be OK, listen to your heart, and EnviroRide will be everything you could imagine and more.

Love,
Gramma

I sat down for six hours and thought about what she said. All I kept saying to myself was that I knew those nasty thoughts were never really me. All that doubt, anger, sadness, jealousy—it wasn't me. I felt as if twenty years of unnecessary misery had been lifted off my shoulders. It wasn't me. When I walked to the store that night I smiled at every person I saw and said, "It wasn't me, the mind poo, it wasn't me!" I'm sure they thought I was a looney tune but I didn't care.

With this theory of Gramma's, Stephen's list of contacts, my old beat-up mountain bike, Lisa and her $60 garage sale bike, and $500 cash from a fundraising party, it was time to start pedaling.

Just Going for a Long Ride

Vancouver, B.C., to Gold Beach, Oregon

Sunday, October 4, 1992. My body felt as if it had been thrown into an industrial cookie mixer. With all the excitement I hadn't got any sleep the past few days. Lisa and I rolled out of bed in the deluxe suite at the Coast Hotel at Stanley Park. The lavish room had been donated so we could start our trip in style. It was gray and cloudy outside with a cool wind blowing the autumn leaves out onto the street. It was eight in the morning and all I could hear in my head was, "You can't do this, you don't have enough money, it's impossible!" I knew that those negative thoughts had nothing to do with me so I shouted back at them, "Shut up and go back to bed, I'm going on the adventure of my life!"

We picked up our bikes from the cycle shop where they had been outfitted with front and rear bags, reflectors, racks, and fenders. Andrew gave us the bill for $340 and told us some non-inspirational stories, like how he had had six straight weeks of rain while bike touring in Oregon.

The Adventures of Coconut Head

LISA

TED

C. H.

We got out of the cycle shop with Andrew's large seed of doubt firmly planted in our mental garden. We raced back to the hotel room and packed our stuff into Ziploc bags to keep our clothes dry. This was my traveling wardrobe: three T-shirts, four pairs of underwear, a Walkman, six cassette tapes, one pair of blue jeans, two sweatshirts, one pair of light pants, one rainjacket and pants, a Hackeysack, a Frisbee, sunglasses, pens, writing paper, Mag-Lite, address book, shoes, a three-year-old mountain bike, and a shitload of ambition. These were the things I wished I had: a tent, a sleeping bag, stove, pots, tarp, food, bike shorts, a camera, and maybe even some money! Then there was Coconut Head. My dad had given him to me as a good luck charm when I moved out of my parent's house. He was a face carved from a coconut and he had traveled all over with me.

We checked out of the Coast Hotel and the media was waiting outside. For the past two weeks I had been on a publicity rampage, mostly radio coverage, and many of the radio stations were expecting us to phone them with updates while we traveled. I had encouraged people to come ride us out of town. Expecting a large crowd of people outside, I opened the doors. There was a reporter from CKNW Talk Radio, six of my friends, and my brother.

Bruce, Andy, Hugh, Tina, Rob, Ted the photographer, and Tom, my brother. This was the big send-off. It all seemed so anticlimactic. My life would be so radically different for the next ten months and I didn't know if I would ever be back. Before we could consider the possibility of never coming back we had to actually leave, but there was a minor detail stopping us. Lisa's front tire was completely flat. I panicked. "A flat, a flat, what the hell is that?" I had never had a flat in my life. Bruce ran

down the street to purchase a new tube and a couple
of patch kits.

This gave us a chance to eat some breakfast.
Sitting in the hotel coffeeshop I thought, "It feels
very safe in here. I'm not really going to ride
from here to hell's half acre, am I? I want my
Mommy!" I pondered optimism: "I believe in
people, I believe the Universe will take care of us,
I believe in all the brothers and sisters everywhere!"

Finally, by 2:00 P.M. we were riding south out of
Vancouver. Tom gave us a ride in his van through the
George Massey Tunnel (no bikes allowed). I shook my brother's
hand and he gave me $100, giving us a grand total of $260.

Now it was really scary. It was just me, Lisa, and Coconut
Head. All I could think about as I rode on towards the U.S.A.
was that we didn't have any money, or camping gear, and that it
always rained in Oregon. I asked myself, "What does that have to
do with now?" Absolutely nothing. Thirty miles south of
Vancouver we arrived in White Rock at my friend Allan's house.
Al, his wife, Linda, and another friend, Sandy, were all very supportive. We slept in the guesthouse and I tossed and turned the
entire night. What the hell had I got myself into?

I was totally exhausted when I woke up, having been on a pure
adrenaline rush for the past week. Sandy gave us a tent to take on
the road with us and we departed White Rock by noon. This was
the first big step: "The Border." The border always freaks me out.
Anything in a uniform gives me the feeling I have done something
wrong. "What is the purpose of your trip?" the lady with the big
head asked. I didn't want to lie so I said, "We're just going for a
long ride!" That was fine with her, which was fine with me.

WE LIVE
THIRTY
MILES
AWAY
NOT
EIGHT!
HA HA

JOE

Right on! The U.S.A.! Fifteen minutes over the border, Lisa had another flat tire. I felt we were lucky her bike had made it this far. I ripped the bike apart, fixed the flat, borrowed a pump from a farmer along the way and we were on the road again.

About four o'clock we phoned my friend Joe in Bellingham. "Hi. We're only eight miles away." "Actually," Joe told us, "you're still thirty miles away." We had to cycle our little butts off because there were only three hours of daylight left. I put some air in Lisa's tire and KAPLOW there went another tire. The second day of the trip and already the stress had started. We had to use duct tape on the inside of the tire to patch it and we headed south full steam.

To make some time we decided to take the Interstate but soon found out that it is illegal for bicycles to be on that part of the highway. The feds pulled us over and showed us an alternate route.

At seven o'clock there were a few concepts that had become realities. Like darkness, hunger, and exhaustion. We continued down the road in the dark with no lights, as our hands and feet turned a tinge of blue while they waited for our arteries to bring some warmth to them. Joe, bless his little heart, came and picked us up because we were taking too long. He and his girlfriend Holly cooked us a lot of food, and treated us like gods.

The next day we headed south towards Everett. We took a secondary highway that ran parallel to the Interstate. There was an unattended apple stand on the side of the road. I hadn't even known that this kind of merchandising existed! I grabbed a Rome apple as big as a cantaloupe, dropped my money in the box and got back on

APPLES

I TRUST YOU

the bike. Riding no hands, listening to Jimmy Buffet and eating a big, juicy apple—this was BLISS!

I was amazed we had already traveled 125 miles. With the sun massaging my face and a light tailwind I felt like I could bike tour forever. We arrived in Everett at 4:45. The Coast Hotel had been very helpful in Vancouver and I had thought maybe they could donate a room in Everett. Unfortunately, they were all booked up. They did make a call to the Comfort Inn and arranged a free room. Again, we were riding around in the dark for half an hour before we arrived. The manager, Bob Beaver, was happy to set us up with a complimentary room. Aaaah, the ecstasy of having a bed to sleep in. Lisa and I were exhausted.

We were on the road by 9:30 that morning and arrived in Seattle by noon. This was our first milestone, the big city! We high-fived and hugged each other because of our great achievement. I tried to swing a hotel room for free. If you want something in this world, you have to ask for it. Well, after spending many hours "asking," we were still homeless. Could it have had anything to do with the way we smelled?

Lisa giggled and said, "This wouldn't be very exciting if we knew where we were staying."

I tried a friend of a friend. Ring . . . ring. "Is John there? You don't know us but we're out for a bike ride. Stephen said we can stay at your house. Do you have any snacks?" "Yes," he said. We had to backtrack five miles across the gun-infested neighborhoods of a large American city in the dark with no lights. Yee-ha!

John lived right beside Green Lake with his mommy and his

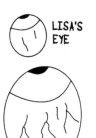

LISA'S
EYE

LISA'S EYE
SWOLE UP
BIG FROM
KITTIES

What
Poo?

WHAT'S
COOKING
HONEY?

A FEVER!

MR. & MRS. IMMUNE

two sisters. A very laid-back dude, he was studying to be a doctor. John pulled out some sleeping bags and let us sleep on the
floor in his bedroom.

Lisa woke up completely stuffed up because of the resident cats
and I woke up with a fever and a migraine. I started my media
blitz anyway. Encouraging people to take care of themselves and
their environment is magnified a thousand times with the help of
radio, TV, and newspapers. The day was spent faxing press
releases about EnviroRide.

I felt sicker and sicker as the day wore on. I retired early only to
find that one of the cats had pooped in my sleeping bag. Oh joy.

The next morning I phoned back to all the media and nobody
had the time of day to talk to me. Now I was freaked, sick as a
dog, practically penniless, paranoid of another kitty surprise, and
the media didn't seem to care about EnviroRide.

Wanting to go home right at that moment, I phoned my friend
Tina in Vancouver. Tina had been a pillar of support for me. She
had helped put the press package together and had organized the
Vancouver media blitz. She juiced me back up by reminding me,
"You have an important mission, just keep going for it!"

I got back on the phone and managed to get a telephone interview with a country station. Without media support, my mission
was useless. I gave my best effort for an enthusiastic interview without fainting from my fever, then collapsed back
onto the bed with a smile on my face, knowing I had done
my part.

Overnight the fever broke. I felt a little better and I
thought John's family was ready for the sick, sneezing,
broke bikers to get back on the highway. We bid them
good-bye and headed out into the unknown world.

Our first stop was a local army surplus store, where we bought a big fat guy sleeping bag for only $89. With the tent Sandy had given us and our new sleeping bag, these two bikers now had a home.

We rode through downtown Seattle past the famous Pike Place Market. They throw fish around like Frisbees before they sell them to you. Both of us were feeling completely unsure of ourselves in this large American city, like a couple of stunned deer running through a field. The only thing that we knew for sure was that we had to keep pedaling.

NO, TAKE ELM STREET

I DON'T KNOW WHERE I AM

Twenty miles south of Seattle I became dizzy and weak from the parasite that was still living in my bloodstream. We found a secluded spot on the side of the road to set up camp. The sun was going down, the ground was made of boulders and our sleeping bag was too small. I know it sounds really glamorous but could I expect this for the whole trip?

We woke up to a beautiful icy cold day blanketed by a layer of fog. In Tacoma by noon, we found the visitor center to get some directions. Most of these centers are operated by retired couples. This retired couple got into a pretty good argument about which way we should go. Unfortunately, their memory lapses overpowered their visitor center skills. We sneaked away without them noticing.

About 150 miles south of the border we stopped in Yelm for a soda pop and the people in the bar really flipped out. One guy was running around yelling, "They rode their bikes from Canada! They rode their bikes from Canada!"

A few miles later we were ready to crash but there were no campgrounds in sight. Our only real option was to ask somebody if we could camp in the backyard. "Over here, Ted," Lisa said, pointing to a little farmhouse. Knock, knock. "Hi, we're riding our bikes around North America. Can we camp in your yard?" I asked innocently. "Sure," the man who answered the door said. Bob was his name and farming was his game. He continued, "But

watch out 'cause I just spread some fresh fertilizer out there." Well, thanks a lot, Farmer Bob. We walked our bikes past a big bull and all the cow stuff to a nice grassy spot, then set up our tent, ate peanut butter sandwiches, and called it a night.

The sound of cows and chickens in the farmyard woke us up. We thanked our host for letting us stay with his fertilizer. He made good toast and shared it with us. His eyes glistened, and his face lit up when he said, "I like farming a lot!"

Lisa and I cycled in amazement down the highway. Bob, a total stranger, put us up for the night and gave us toast. Bob loved his farm. People who love their work radiate health and happiness. I like that.

This bike trip felt like a ride to the grocery store. I was in denial of what was really happening. With our planned route, Miami seemed like it was still 5,000 miles away. That's 'cause it was!

At 11:00 A.M. a headwind blew up. A headwind, what the hell was that? I quickly learned that headwinds and fully loaded bicycles don't go well together. Then some light rain and a few hills. Lisa got mad at me because of all the obstacles. Like I had something to do with the rain, the wind, and the hills. Wouldn't that be cool, if I could control the weather. She laughed at the absurdity of it all and suggested a break.

We found a yee-ha country kitchen and ordered a plate of fries and some water. Lisa passed out while I read the paper. A couple of hours later, the wind had died and Lisa felt better. We continued on through beautiful rolling hills on the winding, turning road.

One hour before dark the strain on Lisa's knee just about had her in tears. Riding all day just about had me in tears too. My ass was incredibly sore. I felt nauseated, and every muscle in my body was vibrating. We knocked on the door of a nonaggressive-looking house, hoping to camp there. John and Lynne let us pitch our tent on the back of their property by the river.

MY BUM JUST TALKED

I AM SORE

The wear and tear from the road has been devastating. There's something about cranking on that bike for seven or eight hours that causes massive confusion to set in. Suddenly I was doing things like walking into the wrong bathroom at the gas station, taking ten minutes to decide on a candy bar, or not paying attention to traffic. We had discovered a new disease, Confused Biker Syndrome.

When the fog cleared from our heads we set the tent up on sand, not boulders, or cow poop. We made a fire while we chowed on peanut butter sandwiches. The nylon tent Sandy gave us was lame. The roof sagged on our faces and it was only five feet wide. We had to use our bike bags to support the corners so it wouldn't collapse. When a breeze hit it, I thought I was sleeping in a wind tunnel. Our beautiful camping spot was a scant fifteen yards away from a railway bridge. I forgot until I was reminded at 2:00, 4:00, and 6:00 A.M.

We got on the road early, ensuring a slow, steady pace into Portland. I wanted Lisa's knee to get better instead of worse. Usually the bike route avoided the major arteries, but parts of

ANTHONY

it included the Interstate. This is where Lisa got a flat. The flat wasn't a problem except for the semi trucks passing by our faces at seventy miles per hour!

We pedaled all day long on the Interstate, focused on trying to stay alive. There was a lot of broken glass and gravel on the side of the road and the traffic was constantly swooshing past us at high speed. We crossed the Columbia River on the massive I-205 bridge into Portland. My friend Anthony, a very warm, wonderful person dedicated to a life in rock and roll, lived here with his blind roommate Tammi. Anthony helped around the house and stayed for free.

It was only about forty-five degrees outside. Knock, knock, knock, open the damn door, Anthony! Nobody was home and we were just about to set up the tent in the yard, when a cool hippie lady came by, "Hey, are you the bikers? Come on in. I don't live here, but Tammi is my cousin." Lori jumped through the window and let us in the door. Tammi came home about ten o'clock.

When she was eighteen years old, Tammi was involved with some kind of dope deal that went bad. The bullet entered the side of her head, severing both optic nerves. She had a little baby boy, Acea, and worked full time as an exotic dancer.

I AM MEXICAN

The next day we stayed horizontal trying to recover from the adverse changes in our lives. Carrying all this weight, the peanut butter sandwich diet, sleeping on strange boulders, and all the other chaos. We slept and played doctor all day long.

October 15, 1992. I phoned the media as soon as I got up. Ring . . . ring, "Hi, we're riding our bikes around North America to encourage people to do their part for the planet." "If I wasn't so busy sorting these paperclips, I would do a story!" they replied.

THANK YOU FOR SHARING

We sent out press releases with little Hershey kisses to every-body anyway.

In the process of delivering the press packages, we had a little incident. Lisa and I were riding into downtown when we were confronted by a very tall man. He jumped aggressively in front of us and yelled, "I am Mexican! I am Mexican!" Hell, I didn't know what to do. He could rob us and make forty dollars, or worse, he could make burritos out of us. I yelled back, "Oh yeah, well we're Canadians!" This confused him and he left.

After the last package was delivered, we found the Democratic head office for Portland. That night was the final debate of the 1992 presidential election. Both the debate and the free sand-wiches sounded like fun.

There was food and TVs as far as the eye could see. When Clinton was on, the crowd cheered. Bush got booed, and, when Perot was on, everybody laughed and took big bites of their sand-wiches. It was like an old vaudeville show.

We stayed the weekend in Portland hoping to get some media coverage. Sure enough Monday morning we got a phone call from Tony at Z-100 radio. He wanted us to appear as guests on the next day's morning show. Then Rob, a friend of Tammi, came over to visit and gave us twenty dollars because he liked our cause. I wanted to take a picture of Tammi, Rob, and Anthony, but I didn't have a camera. Tammi took us out for dinner and refreshments, where we met Steve, another friend of Tammi. He was inspired by EnviroRide and gave us fifty dollars. Between the large donations of cash and being invited as guests on the morning show, I couldn't sleep at all that night. We arrived at the radio station at 6:50 A.M.

Tony greeted us and brought us into the control room. Billy, Tony, Valerie, and Randy kept us there all morning. Their true compassion for our mission was larger than life. We hugged them good-bye and on the way out the door, Tony handed us forty dollars. We were both stunned by his generosity! Then when we got home, Tammi gave us $100 to buy a camera.

We said good-bye to Anthony, Tammi, and Acea. I was moved by the generous people of Portland. We stopped at a pawnshop and bought a Konica 35mm camera and a flash for $150. It was time to face the world and leave the comfort zone.

We headed out of Portland on 99E. Lisa wasn't feeling that well. Going up and down hills with a headwind made for a tough day. We finally made it to Marquam just before dark. Larry, the bartender at the Marquam Inn, gave Lisa free whiskey till she felt better. We knocked at a house just out of town and Holly and Billy let us stay in an empty mobile home on their property.

We were awakened by noisy goats and a cow that tried to eat Coconut Head. In Silverton we chowed on pancakes and got quickly back on the road. Up and down went the hills. Lisa was sick and pooped. I was just pooped.

Around noon, a bee attacked my ankle while I was riding on the highway. I tried frantically to shake the bee off and negotiate

MICHAEL THE
UGLY GOAT

JOHN THE HAPPY
COW FROM OREGON

my bike without going into the busy traffic or into the ditch.

Lisa got another flat so we fixed it up and kept riding through fertile farmland to Marion. At the grocery store we met Jay, who walked us down the street to his house and showed us where we could set up our tent. Somewhere between the tent and Jay's living room we crossed into the Twilight Zone.

Jay, a pleasant man who worked as an alarm installer, introduced us to his family. First there was Grampa Harry. About seventy years old, he confessed to us that he had quit drinking and smoking pot because of his three triple-bypass operations. Then he spit a big wad of black goo into the spittoon. Next was Gramma Grady, a 200-pound gal who had lost her teeth and smoked three packs of cigarettes a day. Then there was David. He was a paraplegic who sat on the couch in the living room. Tucked underneath his legs on the floor was a silver tray that had a big bag of pot on it. The last family member was a bright-eyed and bushy-tailed sixteen-year-old named Scott.

I QUIT
DOPE
BECAUSE
MY LEGS
GO
SMALL

ZIG
ZAG

HAS
ANYBODY
SEEN MY
TEETH?

GRAMPA & GRAMMA

Gramma Grady served us some baked beans, then fresh apple pie and ice cream for dessert. After dinner, Jay and Grampa Harry started talking about Measure 9. Measure 9 was one of the measures the people of Oregon would be voting on in the upcoming presidential election. It was started by a fundamentalist Christian group that believes gay people are freaks and shouldn't have any rights. Voting "Yes" would mean that gays could be refused jobs, health care, and even hotel rooms. "Ya don't want no queers teaching your kids, do ya?" Gramma Grady cackled.

Then the family went into a giving frenzy. They gave Lisa sewing kits and they gave me a really nice watch. Wearing jewelry while riding is really a pain so I gave it back to them. They were crushed and I learned a valuable lesson. When people give me gifts, no matter what they are, I will accept them.

Just before bed Scott told us about his summer job at the llama farm down the block where he cleaned out the stalls and did odd jobs. Odd jobs? What kind of odd jobs? During the mating season, male llamas fight. When they scrap they try to bite each other's special instrument. Ouch! Scott's job was to fix the llama dicks.

We woke up the next morning and got the hell out of hillbilly territory as fast as our little legs could pedal. They were nice folks but they just freaked us out.

We rode in the warm sun all day and stopped at a small house ten miles north of Eugene. Every time we asked people if we could camp in their yard, their faces looked like they had just seen Phyllis Diller naked. Then out of nowhere a couple said yes. When was the last time sweaty strangers from another country asked if they could camp in your yard? Jil and Paul had us in for showers, and stories, then let us sleep in the backyard.

By 8:00 A.M. we were on the road into a thick blanket of fog that covered the highway and the autumn colors of the trees. In Eugene, we found the Saturday Market and I felt as if I were in the sixties. Tofu, tie dye, and hippies with flowers in their hair. Bands played songs with environmental messages, people hugged each other, and there were fresh vegetables too! Bright happy spirits everywhere.

After leaving the market we took a ride out to the University of Oregon. Old, young, fat, skinny, all different kinds of people were cycling. The Oregon Department of Transportation commits 1 percent of all highway funds to building

GRAMMA TAUGHT
ME HOW TO
SEW

SCOTT

PHYLLIS
NAKED

and maintaining bike paths; this was a very bike conscious area. Dave, the afternoon jock at one of the local radio stations, invited us in for an on-the-spot interview.

After more than 400 miles on the road eating nothing but pancakes, French fries, and peanut butter sandwiches, we felt it was time to expand our menu. We both knew that we were supposed to be carbo-loading but we were carbo-overloading. So before we left Eugene we purchased a twenty-five-cent cooking pot at the local thrift store. Then we headed west towards the mighty Pacific Ocean on State Route 126. Lisa was riding too close to me, snagged my bike, and in a second she was talking to the pavement. After I found out she was OK I broke out laughing. It's always entertaining to watch someone do a lipstand.

I used to get distressed when people around me got injured. Then I asked myself, What would help the situation best? Being traumatized or supporting people with love and happy thoughts? Could I be compassionate and not be upset? It's not that I didn't care, I just didn't see any value in feeling bad.

It was getting dark so we found a safe spot to camp down a logging road. A perfect location right beside a mountain stream. We never really asked anybody if we could camp there so we were both on edge, expecting to be confronted at any moment. We set everything up, even a sheltered parking area for the bikes. I built a fire for our first hot meal cooked by ourselves. Dinner was almost ready when we heard very strange noises.

There was full darkness around us and neither of us could see a thing. Lisa freaked out and jumped in the tent. I grabbed a big stick with fire on it. "Come on you!" I yelled. I couldn't tell what it was. It could have been a grizzly, or a psycho high school graduate. It sounded really big, whatever it was. It was crossing the stream only fifteen feet from the tent. I jumped in the tent so Lisa and I could be scared together. The movement went on all night long.

I finally drifted off to sleep, but I awoke to the same sounds. I jumped out of the tent into the daylight. What was it? A bear? A monster? A psycho? No! It was only fish spawning up the creek. I had been scared to death by fish. Both of us had blown things way out of proportion. Have you ever been psyched out this way? We were lucky they didn't come into the tent and slap us to death.

Monday, October 26, 1992. Another foggy morning as we cycled to Mapleton for pancakes and to call our voice mail. We had a voice mail service so our parents could find us while we were on the road. Mariah, the lady who sold us Lisa's bike, had left a message. It turned out the bike we bought for sixty dollars was someone else's. Mariah sold it by mistake and now the owner wanted it back. We were 600 miles away from her, so chances were slim she would be getting it back any time soon.

We were five miles away when we could smell the ocean air. I love the huge rolling waves off the Oregon coast, and hey, it wasn't even raining! We made it to the mighty Pacific and the town of Florence. Time for laundry; all our clothes stank. When bike touring, two things happen to your clothes. They get extremely smelly and sweaty. Then they get stuck in the bottom of your bike bags for a couple of days in the hot sun and they turn into science experiments.

Fish School of Terror

GO AND SCARE THE HUMANS

YES MASTER

BOB BACILLUS

LIVED IN OUR BIKE BAGS

BOB

Outside the laundromat was a "No" to Measure 9 march. Lisa, C.H., and I joined in. There were about 125 lawyers, businesspeople, housewives, teachers, children, people from all walks of life. We marched down the street while the "Yes" supporters drove by yelling, "Faggot Lovers." It was no big deal because I love everybody, even homophobics.

The "Yes" supporters were white high school students. I wondered where they had learned to hate people. Every person, black or white, gay or straight, is just a human spirit with a different kind of body bag. Is it possible for humans to see what's similar with each other instead of what is different?

The state campground had a special biker/hiker area. For only two dollars each we received a shower, some real estate, and total segregation from the large polluting metal things. We met five touring cyclists: Bill and Moira, two actors from Chicago who had already traveled 3,500 miles (that seemed almost impossible), and Carolyn, Graham, and Lisa. They had left Vancouver the day before we had. Someone to relate to! These guys didn't know how to fix llama dicks. We all shared biker stories, then we crashed.

In the morning I checked the voice mail again. There was an anonymous donation of a brand-new tent dropped off in Vancouver. The tent Sandy had given us was small and always seemed to suffocate us by morning. We asked for the new tent to be shipped to L.A. Yahoo!

Florence has long deserted beaches with an unrelenting rolling surf. We walked out to the water in awe of the magnificent environment. Then it was back on the bikes to ride for about four hours, calling it an early day. When we pulled up to the state campground, the ranger told us they had closed for the season fifteen minutes ago. There went our two-dollar camping.

The next state campground was also closed and we continued on to a little grocery store. Virgil, the store owner, showered us with free French fries and told us it would probably be OK to stay in the closed campground. We backtracked and ducked under the fence. Lisa and I played humps on the picnic table and crawled in the tent.

It was freezing cold on the way back to Virgil's store the next morning, where he offered us tea and a pleasant chat. One of the absolute benefits of doing something like this is the social factor. People were always fascinated by people traveling by bicycle. Whether it is the lack of wardrobe, or the challenge of the elements, or stepping into the unknown, there was never a shortage of questions. Pictures with C.H. and we were on the way again.

Even though this highway was set up for bikers, there were a lot of logging trucks blasting by us with great gusts of wind. When two or three went by in a row, the gusts would vacuum us right into traffic. While riding, I focused on survival. Every single day of this journey had brought on a new challenge.

I looked over my shoulder to see a monstrously wide load coming my way. I went for the ditch, but there was only about twelve inches of shoulder, then a guard rail. I scraped up against the guard rail and the wide load missed me by mere inches.

Then there was the "Biker Bridge From Hell" that crossed into Coos Bay. The open water made for extremely strong winds. It was a challenge just walking the bikes over the bridge.

Getting off the bikes slowed the pace down, giving Lisa a chance to notice that her wheel was bent. Neither of us knew why this deformity had appeared. I tried beating the hell out of it to fix it. No matter how many times I kicked or stretched it, it was still warped. We took it to Moe's bike shop in Coos Bay to find out it was only a broken spoke.

Bike Maintenance Lesson #12: One broken spoke throws the whole thing out of whack. Lesson #13: Your foot is not a tool you use to fix a bike. Spokes are only twenty-five cents. We explained to Moe about Enviro-Ride, hoping he would fix it for free. He fixed it and gave us a "special" deal. He charged us seven dollars. Thanks for the bargain, Moe.

HOW MUCH MONEY YOU KIDS HAVE?
MOE

We rode out to the next campground and it was closed, so we took a sideroad to check out the coastline. The Oregon coast looks like an unfinished puzzle, large pieces of rock sticking out, making little jagged islands as far as the eye can see. Colossal waves crashed through tiny itty-bitty holes in the rocks. Watching the power of the ocean, I wondered how those rocks could stand at all. There was a convent of sea lions resting in the late day sun about 300 yards from the shore. The noise level was unbearable, hundreds of them all trying to talk at the same time.

We saw Lisa, Carolyn, and Graham, the three Canadian cyclists, on the road. They had entered the campground illegally so we decided we might as well too. What were we supposed to do, keep riding all night?

Snuggled up in our tent after nightfall there were more noises outside the tent, but this time I knew what it was. Raccoons! Sure I was scared of fish but I wasn't scared of coons. Outside the tent I confronted him. "Go on, get out of here!" I yelled. He looked at me as if I was crazy. I hunched my shoulders and flexed my thighs, but he didn't budge. Defeated, I went back to bed.

It was completely overcast the next morning as we sneaked past the camp host out onto the highway. The five of us stopped at the Breakfast Barn in Charleston. Another cyclist named Aleck, from Tucson, joined us for breakfast and group photos. Aleck, 21, had long hair and a goatee and had been working in Jackson Hole, Wyoming, as a prep cook for the summer. He had left in early September to cycle to the West Coast then back home to Tucson. We all headed south towards Bandon, on Seven Devils Road.

Oregon either has little control over its logging industry or they are just into destroying their forests. Both sides of the road were clear-cut and littered with debris from the process. Most of the Oregon wilderness was so beautiful; what a contrast it was to see a dead pile of lumber in place of it. The road went up and down hill and the odd logging truck thundered by, keeping us on our toes.

AN OREGON FOREST

I HAVE NOWHERE TO BUILD A NEST

I DON'T KNOW WHAT KIND OF ANIMAL I AM

I HAVE NOWHERE TO HIDE MY NUTS

NOW I HAVE TO RENT A HOME

MY STREAM IS DIRTY

We arrived in Bandon about noon. All the other bikers were stopping at the hostelry to stay the night and take a break. The weather outside had started to rage so Lisa and I also decided to stay.

It actually felt good to kick back away from the raccoons, fish, rain, and winds. There used to be so many things I took for granted. Like always having a place to go to the bathroom, to have a shower, a warm place to sleep, or a stove to cook on. Until these little conveniences were taken away from me, I didn't realize how much I appreciated them. We had a chance to visit with everybody, write in the journal, and tell more stories. We met Anja, from Germany. She had started her adventure in New York, had walked and hitchhiked to Alaska, and was now heading to San Diego.

ANJA

Lisa and I had been together every second of every day since September. Want to test a relationship? Just try being together all the time. I looked out the window. The wind was howling and the rain was falling. Inside the hostel, there was no wind or rain. With only thirty dollars left, I phoned Dave (a friend in Vancouver who owed me some money) to see if he could make a payment into my bank account. The elements had taken their toll on my body. My legs were ready to form a union and go on strike. Dave came through and we were able to stay another night. All we did was eat and sleep, eat and sleep.

The next day the rain had stopped and we packed everything up with a burning desire to get back on the road again. Aleck decided to join us, so we had a new riding partner. Just as we stepped outside the hostelry door, the skies opened up. We pulled into the Bavarian Bakery until it blew over and finally got on the road two hours later, with a major headwind from the south.

I WILL BE YOUR FRIEND AND I HAVE A CAMPSTOVE TOO!

ALECK

The Adventures of Coconut Head

The gusts got stronger throughout the day. We were blown to a dead stop going downhill. Yes, downhill! Imagine you are in your lowest gear, putting everything you have into it, then one gust comes up and you just can't move another inch.

This is where I began to question all the things I was carrying on the bike into that wind. Then Confused Biker Syndrome set in. Well, I needed my clothes, but did I really need the tent? I stopped and got rid of a pair of socks, a T-shirt and some writing paper, as if that was going to make a difference. We only managed to do a few miles an hour and it took the life right out of us.

I AM NOT A KITE!

We stopped in Port Oxford for a sandwich feast. There are little things you can do to save money, like borrowing mayo from the deli. Did you know that it takes only 312 little packs of mayo to refill a mayonnaise jar?

We had to fight more gusting winds to make it to the Humbug Mountain State Park. By the time we set up camp we were freezing and the woodpile was locked up. We crawled through the gaps to liberate some jailed wood for a large fire and cooked dinner on Aleck's stove.

October 31, 1992, Halloween. Lisa's knee was giving her increased difficulty. We packed up and rode into twenty to thirty mile per hour headwinds. We had gone only about a mile when sheets of rain started coming out of the sky.

On the right there was a sign advertising cheap breakfasts. Too bad the restaurant was closed. We knocked on the door anyway. A man appeared. "Come in," he said, welcoming us inside. He offered to turn on the grill and cook us up some chow. The Humbug Mountain Inn was active once again.

While he flipped French toast the cook shared his political views. "What we need to lead this country is a good Hitler, not a bad Hitler, but a good one. They're all a bunch of bureaucrats those guys in Washington—for all I know, you could be a bunch of bureaucrats on vacation."

Outside the winds had gained intensity, but with the heavy overcast skies and sheets of rain it was difficult to tell which way they were coming from. After convincing the French toast dude that we were not bureaucrats on vacation, I asked, "Yo, which way do the winds usually blow around here?" "Well, all directions," he said. "Call 'em Whirly Winds!"

Back into the Whirly Winds. We saw a hawk hovering perfectly still above our heads. For five minutes we watched in amazement as he remained motionless in the sky. A couple of miles later we found a fake dinosaur park. (What other kinds are there?) The guide happily told us about a cyclist who was coming down the hill and caught his saddlebag in his front wheels. After doing head-over-heels cartwheels he smeared his face into the pavement, leaving stains on the highway. Thanks for sharing, buddy. Of the 50,000 cyclists who do make the ride down the coast in safety, the locals only tell you about the one that didn't quite make it.

After two hours of radical winds we finally saw the next town, Gold Beach. Lightning started to flash and the three lightning rods on wheels pedaled their asses off to get some shelter. We found a restaurant and joked around with one of the staff members. We told him how everybody told us horror stories about cyclists. Not wanting to feel left out, he told us about how a semi truck steamrolled over a couple of cyclists on the bridge we were about to cross.

The bridge was hairy all right, but we did manage to negotiate it. We stopped at the first café we saw because we were absolutely famished. They served us soggy, greasy, overcooked French fries and soup that tasted like a salt lick. Then the rain set in even harder.

We gave in and got a hotelroom. We grabbed some beer and watched *Star Wars* on HBO. Happy Halloween, Ted. This was the first Halloween in my life I had not participated in. Even when I was an itty-bitty baby my mama had dressed me up. I looked out the window only to see little trick-or-treaters washed away by the flash floods. Every once in a while I could see a clown's head or a witch pop out of the raging white water. Tomorrow would be my twenty-seventh birthday.

Sweaty Strangers
from Another Country

Gold Beach, Oregon, to Los Angeles, California

November 1, 1992. As I awoke that morning in Gold Beach another year older I realized that we had survived the first month and had already traveled more than 850 miles. Lisa grabbed a doughnut from the front desk of our bargain hotel, stuck a match in it, and sang "Happy Birthday" to me. I didn't get any presents except for some gifts from the gods. Rain and high winds. We faced the tropical storm again.

We continued south on Highway 101 over the Thomas Creek Bridge, Oregon's highest bridge. It rained so hard it flowed past my rainjacket and seeped through to my underwear in only a couple of minutes. Then I got a flat, which was impossible to fix in the downpour and that sent us all over the edge. Our only choice was to hitchhike out of there. The first thumb out got us a ride from Bruno and his son, who were out hunting. His son was still shooting his gun out the window while we loaded our bikes into the truck.

The Adventures of Coconut Head

COME ON SON, I WILL SHOW YOU HOW TO KILL

Bruno drove us to Crescent City, about twenty-five miles across the California border, where we met up with Andrew, a friend of Aleck. There was still torrential weather, so we loaded up Andrew's beater VW van with no insurance and motored on through to Arcata. We stopped at the hostel to see if there were any other traveling friends there. Anja, the woman from Germany, was there and donated fifty dollars so we could eat again. A long-term traveler like Anja needs her money to make her trip last. I couldn't believe she gave us fifty dollars. On the other hand, it proved that Gramma Schredd was right. People would take care of us. I just never knew where or when it was going to happen.

When we arrived in the college town of Arcata there were palm trees all around the city square. The palm trees seemed odd in north California because it was rugged logging country with the ocean smacking on its door. I thought maybe I would see some hula dancers or Tattoo from *Fantasy Island* when we got out of the van but it just didn't happen. The four of us split the cost of a hotel room at The Arcata.

BRING ON THE HULA DANCERS' TATTOO

The next day we went back on the road with Andrew and Coconut Head to camp in the Redwoods. The highway took us gradually away from the coastline and twenty-five minutes later we arrived in Humboldt National Park. Riding in a cramped, smelly, polluting vehicle had helped us survive the storm, but I wanted back on my bike.

Outside there were sleeping giants as far as the eye could see. We played Frisbee amid the vast obstacle course. Lisa found a huge tree that had had its base burned out many years before. It was still a living 200-foot monster and was big enough for all four of us to sleep in.

We woke up twelve hours later, after an amazing sleep. From staying in the hotel to sleeping inside a tree was like going from the Ritz to Roots. Andrew went his own way, leaving us to start on a beautiful stretch of highway called Avenue of the Giants. Vehicles were unseen for most of the morning. When the Interstate was built it took all traffic off this popular road. A casual day, stopping to hug trees and admire one of nature's greatest miracles, the Redwoods.

While riding thirty miles an hour down a hill, Coconut Head fell off my bike and managed to roll directly into Lisa's path. She smeared his face into the pavement, just about killing both herself and the Coconut. Luckily everybody was relatively unscathed.

With about forty-five minutes of sunlight left, the sky went bright pink. We were still a long way from Rick and Oja, friends of Stephen in Garberville. Five miles out of town the sun was gone and the sky was pitch black. Riding at night can be fun when you have lights. Too bad we didn't. A vision of what our bodies would look like after a California logging truck pulverized our faces into the dark, unforgiving pavement popped up.

We managed to avoid this fate and arrive safely in Garberville, where the residents were celebrating Clinton's presidential victory.

The next day we did an interview with KMUD, a local community radio station supported mostly by hippies, for the hippies. We always made a point of encouraging people in our media interviews. Blaming people rarely motivates them. If you want people to change the world all you can do is lead by example. Oja demanded that we stay one more day in the hippie hills of California.

MY MOUTH LOOKS LIKE A PIANO

BILL

GEORGE

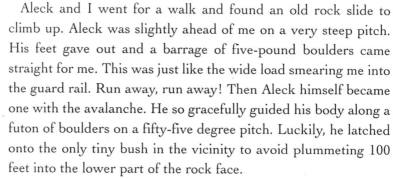

OJA   RICK

THE
CREDITOR

Aleck and I went for a walk and found an old rock slide to climb up. Aleck was slightly ahead of me on a very steep pitch. His feet gave out and a barrage of five-pound boulders came straight for me. This was just like the wide load smearing me into the guard rail. Run away, run away! Then Aleck himself became one with the avalanche. He so gracefully guided his body along a futon of boulders on a fifty-five degree pitch. Luckily, he latched onto the only tiny bush in the vicinity to avoid plummeting 100 feet into the lower part of the rock face.

The next morning we were ready for departure by 8:30 A.M. Rick and Oja live in Humboldt County, also known as "dope growers' county." They gave us a big bag of dope for the road. Then their neighbor gave us a bag of dope. Remembering my pledge about always accepting gifts, I packed it all onto the bike and we said our good-byes.

I checked the budget and we had nine dollars left. A financial donation from the Universe would be most excellent any time now. I checked the voice mail and there were two creditors pissed off at me. Feeling a warm financial glow within me and enough food for a day and a half, we hit the highway.

It was California at its best, warm and sunny. We found a hitch-hiker and gave him all the dope. He was very happy. Then we stopped for a picnic lunch at The Grandfather Tree, a 2,000-year-old, 230-foot-high tree with a circumference of fifty-five feet. Just past Leggett we took Highway 1 to the coast.

It was only fifteen miles to the beach, but the first three miles consisted of the "Hill from Hell." Then ten miles downhill to the California coast. What a ride on a fully loaded bicycle flying downhill into the unknown. The adrenaline was really pumping and we made it to the bottom just in time to watch a brilliant sunset.

Sweaty Strangers from Another Country

It was too dark to go on so we camped illegally in a private campground. We cooked dinner with the light of a candle.

When I popped out of the tent it was maybe 40 degrees with a thick layer of dew encompassing our environment. We tried to stretch some of the kinks out of our beaten, abused bodies on the beach and then we were back on the road again. Six hundred feet of uphill to wake up to and then a screaming hill down. The temperature increased quickly to damn hot. My shoes had been wet for twelve days, giving me dishpan feet, so I tied the shoes on the bike and rode barefoot for a while. We continued south towards Fort Bragg.

As soon as we got into town I heard a distinct sound of a human body and a bicycle crashing to the pavement. Some lady in a K-car opened her door just as Aleck was passing by and sent him flying. He got up and decided both bike and body were fine, and the lady continued on her way like it was all part of a regular day for her. She didn't even stop to see if Aleck was OK. The three of us watched in amazement as she strolled off into the distance.

We rode on to Mendocino and went to Sweetwater Hot Tubs owned by John, a friend of Rick and Oja. It was a very cosmic place with a combined male/female change room. I felt like a male stripper hanging my stuff out in front of strange hippie ladies. I never really understood exactly what hot tubs were for until that night. I turned into a glop of waffle batter.

We camped under a bridge and ate pasta till we exploded. Each day had been a day of discovery, including our eating arrangements. When we flipped our Frisbee upside-down it made a great dinner plate. Three starving people on one plate. Flashes of steel clashing, twisting, turning wrist action to gather as much pasta as my fork could handle before Lisa and Aleck ate it all.

The Adventures of Coconut Head

STILL I AM HUNGRY

ME TOO

YA

MY FACE AT 48 MPH

After riding all day dragging excess weight around I only had one real mission at the end of it: To consume as many calories of energy as humanly possible. Every single night had become an eating contest.

There was beautiful scenery along the California coast to start each morning. Mountains shaking hands with the ocean, gentle slopes, steep cliffs and crashing waves, and on a bike, whoa! The sun was on my face, the sounds of the birdies and the ocean were vibrating my eardrums, and we stopped wherever and whenever we wanted to.

Traveling in a car is totally different. The scenery goes by like you're watching TV. You rarely stop at the things you want to see because you are always trying to make time. The only time you get close to nature is when it passes you by in the rearview mirror. A bicycle is the only way to get the full rush of it all.

What's that I smell? It was a tailwind. Well, it's about time. With 100 pounds of gear I became a thundering wall of flesh, metal, and bananas screaming south into the heart of California. Cycling down a hill I could barely see the speedometer or the road because my eyes were watering. Forty-two, forty-four, forty-six, forty-eight miles per hour. Holy shit, that was fast.

We made it to Anchor Bay and Lisa picked up a women's vibration to go knock at somebody's house for some tenting space. Bill and Connie lived in a simple bungalow on the top of a cliff overlooking the ocean, with their son Adam. We went for a walk on the beach and cooked up dinner.

The next morning our hosts had us in for fresh squeezed orange juice and fresh brewed coffee. Bill's wife, Connie, cooked waffle after waffle. We each had our own plate, much better than the group dinner Frisbee.

Sweaty Strangers from Another Country

Everything went great for three days. Yards to camp in, fantastic weather, and spectacular scenery. Then Lisa's bike starting popping spokes like crazy thirty miles north of San Francisco. The weight of all the gear was too much for the garage sale special to handle. As we rode into Marin County there were five broken spokes on Lisa's back wheel. Her wheel was so deformed it barely turned at all. What's that ahead, honey? Oh I see it now, it's a very large hill.

LISA'S WHEEL

The wheel was so crooked that it made her back brakes inoperable. Big hill, warped tire, and no brakes. I went to the bottom of the hill before Lisa. There was a lot of traffic and potholes, but by now Lisa was an excellent "broken spokes on wheel on bike operator" and made it to the bottom safely. A local bike shop donated the bike repairs and realigned Lisa's wheel for no charge. Moe in Coos Bay would probably have charged us thirty-five dollars.

Highway 101 led us into Marin City. Overwhelming would be an understatement. There were blocks of traffic, screaming drivers, horns, exhaust. We had basically been living in the wilderness for three weeks and were not prepared to be thrust back into the urban jungle. Our loaded bicycles were difficult to maneuver quickly, much to the dismay of the large metal things that were surrounding us from all directions.

We finally arrived at Lori's in Marin City, another friend of Stephen. She showed us where to put our stuff and introduced us to her roommates, all seven of them! They all live together in a communal house. They shared the shopping, cleaning, dishes, everything. At dinner all eleven of us sat down, held hands, and thought happy thoughts to bless the food. Great food and friends always make the spirit sparkle.

Halfway through dinner we discovered that the Lori Stephen actually knew had moved out of this house a year ago. We were having dinner with a different Lori and a group of total strangers. It didn't seem to make any difference to anyone that nobody in this house even knew Stephen.

That morning we headed towards the almighty "Golden Gate Bridge." I was really cranking on the bike. I wanted to see this big bridge, another major milestone of our journey. We stopped for a snack and guess who went riding by — Bill and Moira. They were going to camp at the Marin Headlands. We decided to cross the big bridge tomorrow and joined our friends.

We took pictures of the Golden Gate Bridge (which was painted orange) then headed towards our special little camp spot that was only available for bikers and hikers. These hills were filled with bunkers and old missile launcher units. In the good ol' days of fear, the army used the hills to look out for attackers.

HERE
HE COMES!
RUN, RUN!

AM I
REALLY A
RACCOON?

In the middle of the night I heard the coons at our stuff. I quietly got out of the tent and sneaked up on them. "Aaagh," I screamed. I chased them around butt naked, screaming at them. The coons had gotten into our condiment bag and had eaten all our ketchup, mustard, and taco sauce. Yum, yum.

Sweaty Strangers from Another Country

I eventually got back to sleep knowing that if the Russians did attack in the middle of the night we could blow the hell out of them and any Commie Raccoons with all these here missile sites.

At the first light of day I popped out of the tent. From the campsite looking east the sun painted the sky a warm peach color over the Golden Gate Bridge and the skyline of San Francisco. When we left we had to ride up the steepest hill I have ever had to deal with. The pitch was probably about 15 percent, and with a hundred pounds of stuff, that's a big hill.

We rode south across the orange bridge as a gang of five. On the other side Bill and Moira left and so did Aleck. He had to make it back to Tucson for November 26. Oh no, Aleck was leaving. This wise young man who had a stove was going away.

It was quite a lonely moment. With our last two dollars we bought a loaf of French bread and some Parkay at Safeway. While eating the last supper, Lisa said, "Most jailbirds eat better than we do." It was so damn funny we couldn't stop laughing.

With no place to stay in San Francisco, I phoned my mommy to borrow a little cash to survive on. When your children are eating less than murderers or rapists it's OK to help them out.

We checked into the hostelry. Bill and Moira gave us their stove because they were going home. Things were looking up. We spent the rest of the day playing Frisbee and relaxing. Hostels are really weird places. Everybody is scared of getting stuff ripped off so they all lock everything up. Fear breeds fear.

We awoke very early to update the Portland and Vancouver radio stations. We also managed to find a place to stay thirty miles south of San Francisco in Belmont at Amy's, another of Stephen's ubiquitous friends.

I AM A MASS MURDERER. I EAT THREE NICE MEALS A DAY

The only thing I knew about San Francisco was that Rice-a-Roni was made here and all the cop cars race up and down the big hills so they can smash their bumpers on the road. All kinds of people stopped to talk to us, to say "Hi" or ask us questions. There were happy people everywhere. Surrounded by skyscrapers and business suits, we spent hours on a corner talking and visiting with people.

It was three o'clock before we left downtown and headed south. We managed to avoid most of the huge hills in San Francisco but the bike route took us right through a rough part of town. Abandoned vandalized cars and graffiti on every available surface. Groups of people staring in cold silence as we continued on our way. We passed a grocery store with all kinds of commotion. Fists flying, people meandering into the streets, a man overdosing on hallucinogenic. I kept saying to Lisa, "Stay happy, avoid all fear. Fear attracts more fear!"

POP went Lisa's tire. "Ted, I have a flat!" "Oh no you don't, just keep riding honey," I said. "Ted, I have a flat!" she persisted. Now, if you thought the fish were scary, this was pretty scary too. We stopped and fixed the flat as fast as we could. I moved my wallet to the top of my bags so if someone requested it he could have it easily. We got back on the road with sweaty palms and no problems.

Still ten miles away from Belmont, it was just about dark. Waiting at a stoplight, two businessmen in a car pulled up. Out of the blue they offered us a place to stay and a meal. It seemed odd and yet their offer appeared to be genuine. We declined because we were almost at Amy's.

Sweaty Strangers from Another Country

Amy wasn't home yet so we just hung out at the local doughnut shop. Jose, a hairstylist from across the street, invited us over for free haircuts. We were instant friends. When we arrived at Amy's we met her mom and sister. These were some huge-hearted people, who offered us their home and their fridge.

Lisa and I really needed some time to ourselves. I spent a lazy day in Belmont riding along the shops and checking out the peoples of this suburban community. Lisa spent the day at Amy's sorting, washing, and repacking her stuff.

The next day Lisa and I ventured into an old school that a group of artists was leasing. The staff there surrounded us and I felt like I was in a press conference. The questions came flying from all directions. "How many miles do you go in a day? Where are you going? How come you stink so bad?"

The work of weavers, painters, metal and stone sculptors was everywhere. I could feel the creativity in the air. It was a real awakening experience talking to people "doing their thing." I absorbed all the creative energy that was available.

We hung out for a couple of hours and then Barbara, one of the artists, asked us over for dinner with her boyfriend Michael. Michael and Barbara, a beautiful couple, cooked us an excellent feast and shared their perceptions of America with us. They came across as troopers—trying to help kids in school and reduce violence and dedicated to making the world a better place.

The next day was meet the press day. It was such a thrill to be on the airwaves sharing my insights and experiences with hundreds of thousands of people. I did an interview with

The Adventures of Coconut Head

CBS Radio in San Francisco and updated Vancouver stations CKST and Z-95.

Amy had four girlfriends over to study with and I was surrounded by seven women. They were all talking and listening at the same time, yet every one of them knew exactly what each conversation was about. I needed to go bowling or drink beer or sit around talking about breasts with some guys. I needed to get the hell out of there. I escaped to Village Host Pizza for a Pepsi, caught up my journal, and talked to myself about breasts.

I woke up the next morning with a burning desire to ride Lombard Street in San Francisco, the windiest street in the world. We had to ride thirty miles back into the city but it was worth it. Lombard Street is an incredibly steep stretch of road no longer than a block. It is so steep that hairpin turns were put in to ease the pitch. I finally made it to the top just as my heart felt ready to explode. Riding down was even wilder. We rode over to Fisherman's Wharf only to find massive numbers of tourists and expensive everything.

On the way back to Amy's, we saw a guy with a work for food sign and gave him 10 percent of our cash (one dollar). Our route took us through the same ghetto that had freaked us out so much. This time we didn't listen to the "mind poo" and it was a much more enjoyable experience. It really helped that Lisa's tires decided to keep their air. Sixty-five miles later we had accomplished our mission, had a pizza pig-out, and crashed.

November 17, 1992. Lisa and I were feeling the itch to get riding again. If we sat in the same place for a couple of days we went stir-crazy. There is so much of life to experience! Laundry, pancakes, and then we kissed everybody good-bye. How the hell were we going to survive without phoning mom every time we were out of money? Speaking of moms, Lisa phoned hers to ask for a few dollars. She said she would put it in our account that day.

We had an easy ride in the sunshine, only thirty miles with a tailwind. Most of the scenery was strip malls, gas stations, convenience stores, and fast food outlets. We arrived in San Jose with no place to stay and no campground in sight.

We checked out a few hotels, most of them at sixty dollars a night. We finally found one for thirty-two dollars a night with free movies and as many cockroaches as we wanted. Unfortunately, the bank machine only had two dollars. Oopsie, Lisa's mom hadn't made it to the bank. Time to start asking for some help. The Comfort Inn told us, "Beat it, you hoseheads!" We tried a couple more motels with no luck.

We arrived at the Arena Hotel with really dirty knees from all the begging. Inside we were blinded by polished brass and reflective marble. We spilled our guts: no money, no place to stay, we stink, and the manager, a man named Poova, said, "Yes." The Arena was a brand-new hotel and our room had a jacuzzi in it.

We walked to a Chinese restaurant, ordered chow mein and rice, and danced around the restaurant while the veggies sautéed. We ate our dinner naked in the hotel room. It was truly excellent to stay there; it was the first night we had been alone in weeks.

The next morning we got directions to the radio station from a rather large man in the parking lot. "Turn left at the Burger King, go past the Wendy's, right at the McDonald's, and it's a half a block past the doughnut shop."

At KOME we were greeted by Stephanie, the traffic lady. The two disc jockeys, Bob and Jeff, were glad to have us but the interview spiraled into the depths of nothingness. Bob and Jeff were listing off almost every destination of the whole trip, then tried to make some jokes. I interrupted them, "The reason we are doing this ride is because we think it's really important for people to do something positive for the Earth." They glared at me. I kept going, "Each and every one of you makes a difference." Once I got that out I felt a lot better.

Radio people can have very sensitive egos, and I think I seriously irritated Jeff's. All in all, it was still a fifteen-minute interview on prime time on the big rock station in San Jose. Stephanie gave us a couple of radio contacts in other cities and eight dollars, then the bank machine came through. We were forty-five miles to our next stop—Santa Cruz, on Monterey Bay.

We made it to Highway 17. The ditch beside the road was completely filled with garbage. Why do people do that? We then took the San Andreas Road, away from Highway 17. There was no garbage or debris, just beautiful healthy trees and lush bushes hanging over the road. The pavement curved left and right, then a steady climb uphill through this mountainous area. Climbing uphill really only means one thing, you also get to go downhill. Our hill karma carried us on the magic carpet of descent into Santa Cruz. I love that hill karma. What goes up must come down.

We phoned Mark and Lori, friends of Stephen. They let us drop our stuff off at the house and then we went for dinner. Mark and Lori worked at Kiev, a funky hot tub place. We sat outside in the hot tub peering up through the misty air to see the stars dance across the California night.

Sweaty Strangers from Another Country

That night I had a dream about my dog Betty and my Gramma Schredd. Betty was talking, telling my granny that she was coming out of the closet as a talking dog. Too weird.

With lingering images of Gramma counseling Betty about revealing her hidden secret, Lisa and I headed out on Highway 17. When we arrived in Watsonville it was still another thirty miles to Monterey. It was already one o'clock and we had an interview scheduled with KMBY at 2:30. When we'd started at Santa Cruz we had a tailwind. Now the wind had shifted into a "whirly wind," and Lisa had a sore knee.

I CAN'T LIVE LIKE THIS, I HAD TO TELL YOU!

We finally made it to the radio station around 3:30 and Mark the DJ was really interested in our trip. He gave us a Joe Satriani tape and directions to the campground. It was pitch black when we arrived, then the flashlight died. The ground had a half inch of dirt over rock making it impossible to keep the pegs in. We had to tie the tent to our bikes just to keep it erected. We couldn't have a fire, so we shivered in the dark until we bored ourselves to sleep.

WHAT A DEAL!

Our backs were trashed in the morning from lying on rocks for thirteen hours. Then we had to walk up a steep hill out of the campground since Lisa's leg was still giving her difficulty. Carmel was the first stop, a little tourist town with hundreds of little tourist shops with big tourist prices. We stopped to ask a cyclist where to buy cheap groceries. I had seen this guy before, in Mendocino.

Jacques was his name. "I want to take you guys for breakfast, are you game?" he asked. Another traveler at heart, we swapped stories and he gave us fifty dollars. We bought a brace for Lisa's leg. Groceries, propane, and pictures with the fire department. Only twenty-six miles to Big Sur, our next stop. All along the coast there were huge crashing waves and spectacular rock formations. They looked like little parts of the continent that were trying to run away from home. We made it to the state park with very little daylight left.

It poured rain all night, and every time I woke up, a little more water was rushing into the tent. By morning there were fish jumping inside the sleeping bag. We loaded the bikes up and Lisa had flat #11. This time I couldn't fix it.

The next bike shop was 120 miles away. What will the Universe deliver to us today? We made up some signs: "Dead Bike" and "Will Ride in Back." After a couple of hours a young Texan named Duke picked us up. "My momma told me to never pick up hitchhikers but you folks looked like you was hurting," Duke said. He was as sweet as they come, letting people into traffic and pulling over for faster cars.

He told us how his daddy raised gators and how he remembered tying two cats together and feeding them to the gators. With his smooth Texan accent he laughed at how much fun it was watching the cats trying to get away. Hmmm . . . Duke was a medic in the navy and his assignment for the next week was to have somebody shoot a goat in the training field, then he was supposed to save it. Hmmm.

He went thirty-five miles out of his way to take us to Foothills Cycle in San Luis Obispo. They donated two new tires, a new tube, a patch kit, tea, and cookies. Wonderful people who saved our butts.

Then we were off to the laundromat. We dried the tent and sleeping bags, grabbed some groceries, and rode off into the sunset in search of some real estate. Just out of town we found an old farmhouse occupied by a surfer dude named Tim. He said, "No problem, bikers," when we asked if we could camp by his house and after a good feed it was time to talk to the sandman.

The wind howled all night. I was really surprised that our shitty little tent held up. At 6:00 A.M. I went into the house and Tim was running around in his housecoat with a BB gun and a scope. "What the hell are you doing?" I inquired. "Hunting mice!" he said.

TIM

BORN TO SHOOT RODENTS

As Tim tactically annihilated Mickey and all his cousins we rode through some pretty little California towns, Pismo Beach and Oceana. We stopped in to visit yet more of Stephen's friends, Ron and Nashoma.

Margaret, one of the neighbors, was having a potluck birthday party and we were invited. We arrived at the party meeting all the locals, including the interesting Margaret. We had the usual barrage of questions: "Where are you from? Where are you going? How many miles do you go in a day?"

Margaret instantly became jealous of the attention we were receiving. Margaret, a grown woman, ended up pouting in her room completely pissed off. She figured we'd wrecked her party and wouldn't come out of her room until we left the house. Ted and Lisa, part-time bike tourists and part-time birthday party wreckers.

YOU BIKERS SUCK

MARGARET

The Adventures of Coconut Head

November 24. When we reached our next destination, Los Alamos, we sat around a local bar waiting to attract some beautiful person to take care of us. Ron needed to shave before he could win a beauty contest but he invited us to stay at his house.

Ron went ahead in his car while we rode to Ron's house in the dark. There were absolutely no lights on the road. The only way we could tell where we were was by the feel of the road or the feel of the ditch, a feeling I liked to avoid. Ron was a happy, giggly guy who had lots of homemade wine to share.

We were about 135 miles from Agoura, a suburban neighborhood north of Los Angeles where Dan and Darlene lived, more friends of Stephen. We conquered thirty miles by noon and stopped at a state park for lunch. We had only two dollars left. Being low on funds caused me to panic, always forcing the destination. We chowed on our only food, granola, while we watched the waves crash against the rocks.

When we arrived in Santa Barbara the beach was like a Christmas present. Wrapped up in palm trees, healthy bodies, and sailboats. The Spanish-style housing of the area glowed electric orange from the lowering sun as we searched for a place to rest. We had already cycled seventy miles, the most mileage in a day ever, but we were now out of daylight and no campground for twelve miles. We tried camping in a day park but the ranger kicked us out. Lisa thought we should hang out at the supermarket looking cold and tired so that somebody would feel sorry for us.

No matter how pathetic we looked, nothing happened. We spent one of our last two dollars on a coffee. Desperation set in, so we made up a desperate message. "Two Canadians need a place to tent, can you help?" One hour later a lady named Roxie offered her backyard. She gave us directions, we finished our coffee and we were on the way. Good ol' Roxie forgot to tell us that she lived two miles straight uphill. We finally arrived, stinky and sweaty. We set up the tent. Good night.

In the middle of the night there was squawking outside the tent. We tried to scream, but I thought to myself, "Fish don't squawk!" In a valiant effort I leaped outside the tent ready to conquer. It was a gang of peacocks. They ran away because they were chicken peacocks.

The next morning the sun was shining and the fainthearted birds were nowhere to be found. We rode on down the freeway and made twenty-five miles by noon. But around 2:00 P.M. the wind shifted straight into our faces. Lisa was seriously

TELL ME YOUR PROBLEMS

I LOOK LIKE A PEACOCK BUT...MY INNER BIRD TELLS ME I AM A CHICKEN

lagging behind so we had a deep, intimate talk about going for it in life. We both laughed and cried and continued on our way.

Riding east into the wind continued to be an indisputable challenge despite our mutual pep rally. We were not allowed on the freeway and the bike path went all over the place. We took the freeway anyway so we could make it to Dan and Darlene's that month. Two minutes on 101 and we were busted by the feds. Earlier we had phoned the highway patrol but they had no idea where bicycles were supposed to ride. The cop that pulled us over gave us great directions on how to get to Agoura and within a few minutes we were back on our way into the King Kong winds.

With thirty miles to go and only a half hour of daylight left, we had to stop. Jeff and Barb, a heavy Christian couple with a new baby girl and a cute little farmhouse, were happy to let us camp in their yard. They gave us Oreo cookies and told us of their disgust for Clinton's plans to give homosexuals human rights and his weak foreign policy. Whatever happened to "Love thy neighbor" and "Thou shalt not kill?" I guess that only applies to some Christians, or only when they want it to.

Early next morning we departed on Portreros Road up a really, really, really steep grade. Did I mention it was really steep? It was almost too difficult to walk up with all the weight. We finally made it to Thousand Oaks. The weather had warmed up. T-shirts and shorts during the day and then cool at night. The locals were all bundled up in ski jackets once it went below 80°F. We had a short nap and the flies were swarming. I guess we smelled worse than I thought.

We arrived at Dan's in Agoura, putting the mileage total for the trip at 1,723. Their beautiful house had lots of windows and bedrooms and was nestled in between the rolling dry hills of the area. About 6:30 Jeannie, their neighbor, came over and was absolutely stunned at what we were doing. She ran home screaming, "I'll be right back, you poor kids!" She came running back screaming, "I was going to give these to the homeless but, but you guys need these pumpkin pies more!" Absolutely flustered, she continued, "and here's ten dollars, it's half of what I've got."

The next morning, Dan and Darlene offered to be town guides around L.A. While they were getting ready we opened our mail, which we'd arranged to pick up here. Lisa received her sandals from Vancouver, my mom mailed some pictures and Amy, a friend from Wham-O, sent us six Frisbees. Great, more plates, I thought. There were supposed to have been some donations but they must have been mailed somewhere else. We also received our new lightweight awesome tent. There was no note, no clues to where it came from, just a new $300 tent.

After exhausting all the possibilities on the mail front we hopped in the van and drove into Los Angeles. We stopped at Universal Studios for a look. There were TOO MANY PEOPLE and it scared me! Blatant tourism in every direction. Lineups for the bathroom, screaming children, T-shirts, postcards, yuk. We stopped by the Walk of Fame and all the people from Universal had got into their vehicles and raced there before we did. Large groups of bewildered tourists equipped with extra shopping chromosomes are best left to themselves. We stayed in the van where it was safe.

I couldn't believe how damn big the place was. The images of this town being raped and pillaged from the Rodney King riot in 1992 were still fresh in my mind. I wondered how many of these people were armed. Lisa and I realized that neither of us had any interest in discovering the streets of Los Angeles. We made it home in one piece and chowed on a big feast. Dan had an old player piano that he pumped with his legs. We sat around singing songs and laughing the night away, happy to be far from the large oozing city.

Next morning we went to Kinko's to photocopy some more press releases. We had to borrow fifty dollars from Darlene so that we could exist. We spent the whole day writing letters and stuffing envelopes. We sent out ten bike sponsor packages because Lisa needed a new bicycle. Her sixty-dollar touring machine sucked potatoes.

The next night we saw Darlene around dinnertime and she had a surprise for us. That day she had talked to a friend of hers named Arnie, telling him about our adventure. That night we were going to visit Arnie, who wanted to give us a bike.

We had to go east on the freeway to get there. Ten lanes of yuppies in BMWs and Porsches racing to get here and there. The freeway was like a monster, large, dangerous, and frightening.

Twenty minutes later we arrived at Arnie's. We couldn't get a single detail out of Arnie as to why he wanted to give us a bike. All he did was ask questions. With each detail of the trip that we explained he became more and more shocked. It was funny to watch his face and see the bewilderment it was expressing. He took us to his garage and gave us a mountain bike that had been used only a handful of times. It was getting to the point where whatever we needed just showed up. This donation was nothing short of a miracle. He threw in a Swiss army knife and a handlebar bag.

His wife, Denise, came home. "Honey, these are a couple of Canadians that I just gave my mountain bike to." "You mean the bike I can't even touch, you are giving to two total strangers?!" I think Denise was more shocked than we were. Lisa had a new bike.

FREEWAY BOY

THE NEW BIKE

Journey into the
Big Ugly Monster

Los Angeles, California, to San Diego, California

December 1. Our next challenge was to make it out of Los Angeles alive. All the stories of gangs, guns, and violence were being broadcast live in my head. Luckily we had some friends and family to stay with as we attempted to negotiate this land of what Gramma Schredd called "mind poo."

Lisa woke up thinking she had just dreamed about a new bike. However, the bike was still sitting in Dan and Darlene's garage where we had left it the night before. We changed all the racks and the water bottles over from the garage sale special, making Lisa's new bike ready for action. We had created a new bicycle from out of the blue. It was a day of cleaning, polishing, and oiling.

Susan from Quantum Leap called, asking if I would be able to speak at the Quantum Leap Christmas seminar in San Antonio. Quantum Leap is a course designed to encourage people to reach their full potential. I had taken the seminar in Vancouver two

GRAMMA
SCHREDD

years before and had kept in contact with Susan and her husband, Craig, while I was traveling. Susan offered to fly me out to San Antonio and Lisa could stay at her house in San Diego while I was gone.

The news that night made much of the fact there was rain in the forecast. The Los Angeles media treated the rain like a natural disaster. Updates in the middle of TV shows every five minutes, as if the end of the world were around the corner.

An early morning sprinkle began as we departed Agoura to tackle the streets. We were on our way to Kathleen's, another woman involved with Quantum Leap. Our bikes took us east on Ventura Boulevard—twenty-five miles of McDonald's restaurants and palm readers—past Universal Studios, Warner Brothers, and Disney Studios.

When we arrived, Kathleen showered us with hugs and kisses. She was a sweet kid who plays full out and had the same philosophy as us—have as much fun as possible every minute of every day.

At half past five that evening, there was an earthquake, and another at nine. "What's that shaking?" I asked shakily. "It's an earthquake," Kathleen said unshakily. These Californians are hilarious. They treat earthquakes as if they were as common as a cup of tea, but when it rains, "Get the children inside! Cancel work! Panic buying of groceries!"

In the morning I phoned the media, got contact names, wrote letters, and made a delivery list. Kathleen got home at 1:00 P.M. from her job as a breast examiner and we got in the car and grinded it out in traffic to deliver the press releases. We saw NBC, Fox, and CBS. All three of us became totally stressed because of the gridlock rush hour.

Journey into the Big Ugly Monster

The next day we felt we had to try the tourist thing. After all, a short five-mile ride from Kathleen's house and we were in the land of the stars. At Grauman's Chinese Theater in Hollywood hundreds of people were wandering around looking at handprints.

WHERE ARE ALL THE STARS?

I can only handle tourists for a short period of time. What kind of a holiday is it to be jockeying through people all day to see who has the best-priced T-shirts? People buy the shirts to remember what they missed because they were too busy buying T-shirts. I was surrounded by T-shirt shoppers.

WHERE CAN I BUY A SHIRT?

All this tourist thinking must have had some subliminal effect because I awoke the next morning saying, "We must climb the HOLLYWOOD sign." We screamed through Hollywood to get to the big letters on the hill. After a half tank of gas we made it to the base of the sign. Excitement and euphoria.

But as we got out of the car we noticed the signs everywhere: NO CLIMBING THE HOLLYWOOD SIGN – $103 fine. What's the three dollars for? We glanced upward to those historic letters and considered doing it, but the parked car would have been an obvious tip-off to our plans.

So we went to Beverly Hills to have a look at the mansions. Huge houses blocks long with many rooms, fountains, limos, and BMWs. Why would anybody need thirty rooms? The "Use only what you need" game is obviously not played in Beverly Hills. Enough of this car ride, I wanted to ride my bike. Kathleen put twenty dollars in our pockets and sent us on our way.

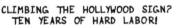

CLIMBING THE HOLLYWOOD SIGN? TEN YEARS OF HARD LABOR!

Thirty miles away in Monrovia lived a friend of mine, Amy, who worked for Wham-O. On the way there Lisa and I passed through Pasadena and there were bleachers on both sides of the road. It was for the upcoming Rosebowl Parade. We felt like we were on parade the way everybody in this trendy California town was glaring at our loaded bicycles.

When we arrived at Amy's, her fiancé Steve and their neighbor Ruth were outside drinking wine and cheering us on. A welcoming committee. Amy and Steve were very excited. They cooked us dinner, fed us chocolate and we all shared happy thoughts. They slept on the couch so that we could crash on their bed. I can still see Steve cramped in the fetal position telling us he liked sleeping that way. Steve and Amy had hearts as big as football stadiums.

Our plan had been to leave for Anaheim after a good night's sleep but there was a torrential downpour happening outside. Amy invited us to the Wham-O head office for a tour instead.

Upon our arrival, Amy presented us with a handmade rainjacket for Coconut Head and then we went for a tour of all the Wham-O toys over the last couple of decades. She apologized about the disarray of the display cases, saying that the last earthquake was to blame. There were slingshots (where they got their company name from), Sillystring, Frisbees, and more. It was a refreshing walk into my childhood past.

That evening back at Amy's, Lisa and I jumped on the couch and pretended to be asleep before Steve and Amy insisted that we sleep in their bed again. I was beginning to get uncomfortable with people providing for us. I was too scared to go outside in this gargantuan metropolis, but we had cycled only fifty miles in the past ten days. It seemed as if we were just hanging out so people could feed us. I didn't like that; we had to move on.

Steve and Amy had left for work by the time we got up and had left a twenty-dollar donation to EnviroRide on the table for us. We took the bike path that went all the way to Anaheim down the Santa Ana River. Yesterday the area had been completely flooded, but the water had receded enough for us to give it a try. There was slimy mud, sand, sticks, and debris littering the path. Going under a bridge, I had to lift my feet up just to get through the puddle of water that was licking at the bottom of my bike bags.

We didn't have a lot of choice. It was this or the streets of East L.A. We strolled through the fresh morning smog, with the captains of industry on both sides, their smokestacks belching pollutants into the sky. In between the bike path and the buildings were six-foot fences topped with layers of barbed wire.

City crews had locked up the gates the day before to keep people away from the flooding river but they had forgotten to unlock them today. We had to hoist our fully loaded bikes over the six-foot fence. Only a hundred yards later we came upon another locked fence. We took our bags off the bikes, and this time climbed underneath. The trail took us right onto the concrete riverbed, just like in *Terminator 2*, but Arnie wasn't there.

The Adventures of Coconut Head

Yesterday's watermark was three feet high on the riverbed so we knew we'd been darn lucky that we'd stayed at Amy's an extra day. We finally made it to the turnoff and had to lift our bikes over the fence again to get off the bike path.

We arrived in Anaheim about 7:00 P.M., at Brenda's house, Lisa's cousin. She was warm and friendly and, to our surprise, worked at Disneyland in the accounting department. She quickly offered to get us in the gates the next day.

The first thing I thought when I woke up was, "I'm going to Disneyland to see Mickey and Goofy and all the fellas!" I needed the camera but when I reached into my bike bag to grab it, my hand came out red. There were thousands of ants everywhere! I lifted the bag up and found a rotting orange inside. The ants went marching one by one hoorah, hoorah! I guess it was time to clean the bike bags.

After cleaning that up I took an apprehensive look at my bike. My rear tire had had very little tread on it when I started and now it was completely bald. With three patches, it was ready to ride again. We had been waiting for some cash to show up but we had only one dollar in our pockets and no money in the bank.

Disneyland was almost completely devoid of people when we got inside. We ran from ride to ride with the greatest of ease. Space Mountain, Splash Mountain, The Matterhorn, Fantasyland, What A Blast! This is a place that takes great pride in the product they offer and I was highly impressed. The employees of this company were truly in alignment with Walt Disney's vision. Disneyland: a place where children of all ages can play in a safe, fun environment. What a contrast from the lovely bike path that took us to Brenda's house.

We went outside the gates to our bikes, and my tire was flat again. I patched it but we had to walk to the closest gas station for some air. We had spent our last dollar on a drink in the park. What do you know, it costs twenty-five cents for air. Begging for food is one thing but begging for air is something else. Some guy laughed in my face and tossed me a quarter.

The next day we rode on to Costa Mesa where Lisa's Uncle Murray lives. The only scenery we had that day was constant suburbia. As soon as we arrived Murray had our bikes up on the repair stand. He cleaned all the grease off, oiled things up and discovered that my bike had a broken frame. That was bad. Murray had a friend who was a welder. That was good.

Murray was up at 6:00 A.M. and out the door to have the bike welded. KROQ had phoned, asking if I'd do an interview with the Doc on the Rock, one of L.A.'s biggest radio stations. Being on the air in L.A. meant a potential audience of millions. I always kept my interviews positive but in this one I got a little message out to the politicians in L.A.:

"The smog problem here is ridiculous and there are no bike paths. The one path we found here was chained up. Let's make it as difficult as possible for people to ride their bikes. Come on! Look, I will even help you. I will go to K-Mart, buy some paint, and make some bike lanes. The planet won't be any fun any more if we're all dead!" So said Ted Schredd.

That afternoon Murray came back with the fixed bike. I was thankful that he had been so attentive to the needs of my machine. Then he took us to Performance Cycle because something was screwed up on my back bearings. John the mechanic saw the condition of my back tire and told me to come see him on Monday.

We took it easy for the weekend but first thing Monday I called John the bike mechanic and he told us to come on down. He gave us two tires plus tune-ups, cycling gloves, pants, and ten dollars. A real sweetheart.

The *Daily Planet*, the local newspaper, met us at Murray's house for an interview. The reporter was sure that the next time she saw us we would be on Letterman. Murray escorted us out to the highway, hugs, kisses, and we were on our way to San Diego to Susan and Craig's house.

We left Costa Mesa south on Highway 1. It felt great getting away from Los Angeles. It left me feeling disillusioned about how anybody could see value in living in this less than inspirational area. We only cycled maybe twenty-five miles that day into Dana Point.

We only had two dollars and a campsite was fourteen dollars so we had to sneak into the campground. It had been three weeks since we had camped and this was the first time we had a chance to set up our new tent. It dropped to 40°F so we put on every layer of clothing we had but we were still shivering.

A couple in a VW van from across the way came to visit. Matt and Kelly, from Pennsylvania, had traveled across the States in search of a warmer climate. Lisa started bragging about my trip to Texas for the Quantum Leap convention. Matt had been sharing some wine with her and I think it went to my sweetheart's head. I just stood back and watched. For the last couple of weeks I had had expectations of how she should be. Suddenly, I had no more expectations.

US
BEING
COLD

Journey into the Big Ugly Monster

In that moment I knew I had changed. Lisa was free to do whatever she wanted. If her knee wanted to hurt or she wanted to get mad at the elements that was OK with me too. We crashed out when the fire died.

We were up at 7:00 A.M. and got out of the campground before the ranger found us. We bid Matt and Kelly farewell and headed south to Encinitas.

I JUST PUT THIS CREAM ON MY THIGHS AND THE FAT MELTS RIGHT OFF

CREAM

ALL THE CHICKEN YOU CAN EAT

The southern part of California just doesn't have the charm of the north. Everywhere we looked there were the signs of massive overpopulation: the smog, the water shortage, and the constant barrage of fast-food outlets. Unnaturally obese people, guns, crime . . . obviously something was out of balance here.

That night we stayed with another Quantum Leap contact, Melvin in Encinitas. Melvin had an orange tree right in his backyard. We had fresh squeezed orange juice, steamed potatoes, and zucchini for breakfast. Melvin went to work and we continued south.

Just outside of La Jolla there was a fairly big hill to climb. Once I started, I noticed there was another cyclist a couple of hundred yards ahead of me. Even with all my weight I was able to pass this guy before I got to the top. It was a "Ted Testosterone" moment.

Heading into La Jolla we went down a 700-foot hill that took us right to sea level. We screamed all the way to the bottom—it's a great way to express yourself and get some attention.

We got to Craig and Susan's house overlooking the ocean. A house where you could watch the beautiful Pacific sunset through the silhouette of the palm trees. They were away until Saturday so Lisa and I had the whole pad to ourselves.

The Adventures of Coconut Head

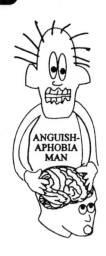

ANGUISH-
APHOBIA
MAN

GOSH, I REALLY
SCORED BIG ON
PRESENTS!

I DIDN'T
SCORE
AT ALL

A couple of days later they returned with big hugs and kisses. The very next day Craig left to go home to Houston for Christmas. I left the two women at the house, needing some time to myself. I felt a change coming on as if something really great was going to happen. Perhaps one of the bike sponsors would come through. Lisa had a new bike; maybe I would be blessed with one too. I rode into town to find a bar with a bunch of guys around. Beer, football, and pictures of women's breasts on the wall. Sometimes a guy needs to just be out with the guys.

I made spaghetti for Lisa and Susan the next night, serving it up with fancy linen and candles while we played the Elvis Christmas album. Lying in bed I was feeling mentally anguished. I had Anguishaphobia! Maybe it was because we had only cycled 300 miles this month, or was it the lack of money, or because the next stretch of the ride would be desert for the next couple of months?

Susan left the next day for her Christmas in Texas. I would meet up with her and Craig at the seminar. The deck outside their back door provided a theater of nature. That night we were splashed in color as we watched the big blazing hydrogen ball from the sky drop below the horizon while the palm trees waved good-bye. Sunsets are an excellent time to consider the intricacy and splendor of the world we live in.

Wednesday, December 23. I picked up a package at the post office from my mom. I quickly opened the two presents from the package only to realize that one of them was for Lisa. Lisa had got only one present and I had opened it. There was a sweatshirt each from my mom and Lisa's mom put 150 Christmas dollars in our account.

The next morning the camera jammed and I was desperate to get it fixed. Christmas was tomorrow and it took numerous phone calls to find someone who would even look at it. Rich, the camera dude, was not encouraging. "Looks like you're gonna need a new camera because these gears are all jammed!" "That's not possible, you see we're on a budget and buying a new camera just isn't affordable." Each day had such bizarre and unpredictable experiences, how could we be without a camera?

MUST FIX CAMERA

Five minutes later he showed me a piece of sand that had been caught between the gears. He also soldered my broken battery pack. Now there was no need to buy a new camera, but I prepared myself for the repair bill. "No charge!" he said. Damn it, there was a Santa Claus.

The very first street person I saw, I slipped him a five spot. I was so excited I phoned Lisa to tell her the great news. I told her to meet me at the local coffee shop. On the way there I was thinking, what can I buy Lisa for Christmas—and it hit me. Every year of my life I have become miserable about Christmas and miserable over the pressure of buying for others. People give because they are forced to, instead of giving from the heart! Christmas has become an exercise in blatant consumerism around the world. Lisa and I gave each other presents all the time. Giving is about being free, not because you are supposed to. Besides, I'd rather have food than presents.

HI YA, HI YA!

TRANSLATION:

(KILL THE BIRD, AND LET'S HAVE SANDWICHES)

I met up with Lisa at the restaurant. Matt and Kelly, the two campers we had met last week, also strolled in. We pooled our cash and made a group decision to buy a turkey; I had an awfully big craving for a turkey sandwich. It was a busy day in the supermarket and also a busy day for free samples. Us bikers had this down to a science, eating as much free food as possible. Lisa bowled cans of beans at me while I ate all the free snacks.

CHRISTMAS

SEALS

After Indian leg wrestling with the turkey to defrost it, I engaged in hand-to-hand combat to get it into the oven. It was obvious I had been out of the domestic scene for a while. When I started the dishwasher there was no soap, so I used dish soap. The dishwasher began puking up buckets of foam all over the kitchen. While this was happening, something began flaming in the oven, and smoke was engulfing the kitchen, triggering the smoke detector. I panicked and knocked a glass into the sink, breaking it into tiny crystals. I paused and thought, action cooking!

Christmas Day. No presents, no tree, no snow, no Santa, it just seemed like another excellent day. Lisa and I spent all morning on the phone touching base with our families, then Lisa and I went to the beach, played Frisbee, ate turkey sandwiches and watched the seals swim by. It was the first Christmas in my life without snow, but huge rolling waves and beautiful palm trees is not a bad thing.

Nikki came at 8:30 the next morning to take me to the airport so I could catch a flight to San Antonio, Texas, for the Quantum Leap seminar. I was excited about leaving; I needed a break from Lisa. Our relationship seemed to be deteriorating. Maybe the time apart would give me a chance to appreciate her more.

Hot damn, I liked plane rides. The flight took about three hours; to ride my bike there would have taken about two and a half months. I arrived at the airport and was greeted by a whole bunch of happy, shiny people. They got me checked into the hotel room and as I lay in bed I knew how great it felt to be by myself.

The next morning I met some of the speakers and the seminar participants. There were many attractive women there and I thought back to what had attracted me to Lisa in the first place.

Yes, she was beautiful but it was her smile, her warm glow. I realized that I, the bike guy, no longer chose a woman by her physical features. There is only one thing that magnetized me now, a woman's energy. Any shape or size of woman with a positive energy about her, and wham out go the vibrations of attraction. One woman from Austin, Texas, named Deanna particularly caught my eye. The attraction was instant and I asked around to find out where she was from. I set my intention for this girl to cross my path.

At 6:00 P.M. the next evening the unfolding of the Universe began. I was sitting in the lounge waiting for dinner, Deanna showed up, and I started the idle chitchat.

The conversation flowed for six hours straight. I can't even remember what we talked about. All I can remember was how much I was in awe of Deanna. She was bright, smily, funny, happy, giggly, and sexy. I was in awe yet I felt an incredible sense of calm and tranquility around her. When we finally realized what time it was, we hugged each other and called it a night.

The next morning, feeling charged up from my conversation with Deanna, I found David, an incredibly enthusiastic five-year-old. He chased me all over the resort, giggling with glee, lost in the moment. I giggled with glee, too! We were both having max fun.

A lot of parents give toys to their kids, toys to express love. I think spending time with someone is the best way to express love. Who is the child's best friend, his family or his Nintendo? Am I crazy with this theory? Am I toyaphobic? Should I get help?

As my toyaphobia decreased so did the sunshine and we finished the day of seminars with a bonfire. I saw Deanna and asked her if she wanted to go on a walking date with me the next morning. She agreed.

THIS IS FUN

PARTS OF ME
ARE BOUNCING

We met just outside the conference center, which was surrounded by a golf course on one side and rolling hills on the other side. It was about 65°F with an overcast sky. After some quick breathing exercises to get the oxygen going we ran up a hill that overlooked the resort. Halfway up Deanna asked me, "Do you want to hike naked?" After I recovered from the shock, I thought, how could I say no to a question like that?

Up on the hill we ran around, screaming and dancing among the trees. What an incredibly, freeing experience it was to hike naked. My body was in total bliss and ecstasy. As we started our hike down we noticed our clothes were an awfully long way away. On top of the hill we thought nobody would be able to see us. When we got to the bottom we realized that everybody could.

The seminar participants were on their way to breakfast when we walked by them in the other direction fully clothed once again. Even though I was extremely dirty and sweaty, I felt an incredible sense of euphoria. I felt I was one notch short of levitating.

All morning back in the classroom, I felt like someone was pumping me full of bliss. At lunch time I was standing in the buffet line with Deanna. "You hungry?" I asked, "Not, how about you?" she replied. I said, "Not." Without a second to spare we blew off lunch and ran back to the room ripping our clothes off touching, feeling, exploring. Ecstasy was running through my bloodstream.

That afternoon I made a presentation about EnviroRide, encouraging people to be the most they could be and to really go for it in life. They gave me a standing ovation and the donations started flying from all directions. Places to stay, new sleeping mats, cycling shorts, and more than $400 in cash. With the combination of Deanna, the response to the talk, and all the donations I levitated to the front foyer of Cloud Ten!

That night was the New Year's Eve party and I was asked if I could help emcee the talent show. I borrowed a $1,300 Italian suit from Kevin, one of the trainers, a suit worth more than my bike and all of my possessions combined.

At the party everybody was dancing, loving, hugging, and kissing each other. We had put up half the talent for the show before midnight but it was now 1:00 A.M. and people were still dancing. I was scheduled to leave in less than twelve hours so Deanna and I disappeared into the night back to the hotel room. Making love to Deanna was absolutely magical. Passionate, gentle, sharing, and exciting.

I drifted off to sleep knowing that Deanna, this hotel room, and the whole experience was coming to an abrupt end.

Change Your Partners
Do-Si-Do

San Diego, California, to Tucson, Arizona

January 1, 1993. I said good-bye to everybody and Deanna drove me to the airport, where we had wild sex in the back seat of her Honda in the parking lot, in broad daylight. I will remember forever Deanna's departing words, "Well, it sure was nice meeting you, Ted!"

It was an incredibly long plane ride back to San Diego thinking about Lisa and Deanna. I felt I had to tell Lisa what had happened because I am such a shitty liar and she had a right to know. As soon as we were alone together I told her about Deanna and the connection we had.

All I could say was that it had just happened. I had never intentionally left San Diego looking for a new love. We talked for about four hours before Lisa drifted off to sleep.

I didn't sleep at all that night; I just lay there wide awake for hours. At the first light of day I went for a walk to figure out what the hell to do. Ten minutes into the walk I confirmed that I wanted

Deanna. I immediately phoned her. "Do you want to quit your nursing job, sell your car and all your stuff, fly to Tucson and start riding with me?" With only a moment of hesitation, she said, "OK. I just bought a new bike last week. I might as well get some use out of it."

I was elated and depressed at the same time because now I had to tell Lisa, my partner, my buddy, my lover, that I wanted to go on without her. What was she going to say? She had no money. How was she going to get home? Could I make it to Tucson by myself? My head was reeling, my heart was aching, and my soul was doing cartwheels down the street. I put my seatbelt on for the upcoming emotional rollercoaster.

As soon as I walked in the door, Lisa knew what was going on. It just seemed to spew out of my mouth: "I'm sorry but I no longer want to ride with you." At this point you are probably thinking that I am a "Wiper of Other Babies' Bottoms" for doing this to Lisa. But I had to go with my heart and not my head. Lisa and I had had a great relationship at one time, but things had changed on the road. It was a difficult thing to do, but to take the path of least resistance by staying with Lisa would have been much more painful. Lisa went into a state of shock.

She had gotten me this far. Without her who knows what could have happened. There was a reason why Deanna had showed up and I had to keep in the flow of what was going on. All day long I cried, Lisa cried, I cried, she cried, we cried together. I had gone from Endorphin City in Texas to the Bowels of Hell in San Diego in just a few hours. I knew that this was a test of spirit for both of us. Lisa was physically ill, nearly vomiting a couple of times. As the reality of the whole situation set in, I began to break through the sadness, knowing that I had made the right decision. We both lay in bed wide-eyed with nothing to say to each other.

We went to the beach the next morning to clear up some left-over feelings. Lisa cried more. I encouraged her to release whatever anger she had for me or Deanna. She called me a jerk and Deanna a slut, which seemed to make her feel a little better. I gave Lisa some money, then she phoned her dad for a plane ticket and made plans to fly home with the new bike on Tuesday. It was time for me to move on.

I decided to blow off the media in San Diego until I had mentally sorted things out. Craig and Susan drove me to a campground that was 3,200 feet in elevation near Live Oak Springs east of San Diego.

As they pulled away I was overwhelmed by silence. It had been months and months since I had heard complete silence. Every part of me felt calm and peaceful. It was chilly as I set up camp. I made coffee, then went to the phone and called my mom to explain to her what had taken place. She was both shocked and supportive.

I phoned Deanna and had spiritual orgasms just talking to her on the phone. She told me that her car was sold, she had quit her job, and she was ready to meet me in Tucson in about three weeks. Deanna was concerned about being able to keep up. She had rarely exercised, had never been camping, traveling, or without a shower in her life. I wondered if she would be able to handle eating boiled potatoes for five days in a row.

After three hours on the phone it was really cold outside. I put on every piece of clothing, including hat, gloves, and socks, that I owned. I was still freezing. I went

THAT FELT REALLY GOOD!

A SPIRITUAL ORGASM

outside the tent to get some water and my water bottles were frozen solid. Back in the tent I was lighting the camp stove every ten minutes for heat. I enjoyed sucking propane fumes as icicles dripped off my nose. I went to bed at eight o'clock hoping it would warm. Not.

When I woke up the next morning I was surprised I was alive. I had to pull my hat over the tip of my nose and my sweatshirt over my head. It was a balmy 17°F. Right then and there I set my intention for a warm place to sleep that night. That day on the bike I climbed three 4,000-foot summits. The bike was extremely heavy with all the extra weight from the sleeping bag, stove, food, tools. The stuff that Lisa used to carry.

The "Celebrate Good Times" song by Kool and the Gang kept humming through my head. I had one more summit to go then ten miles of 6 percent grade downhill, right on! Forty-five minutes of spectacular descent past beautiful mounds of earth-tone stone that looked like millions of small rocks piled 4,000 feet high.

Just off the highway I found a yard in Ocotillo to camp in. The owner, Bob, had a better plan for me, a heated motorhome with a stove and a nice desk to work at. I worked five hours that night and three hours the next morning relaying my feelings to my journal about Lisa leaving and Deanna joining me.

My excitement about seeing Deanna was mounting, but would she be able to handle life on the road? I loved Lisa and leaving her behind was extremely difficult. Had I made the right decision? My heart felt like it had been slammed in a car door. I had nobody to confide in but myself.

As I rode by the sheriff's office I saw a scare tactic poster to deter people from traveling through the desert. I had 1,500 miles

DON'T DO ANY THING

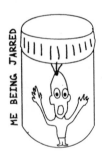

ME BEING JARRED

NOT EAT MUST SLEEP

of desert ahead of me before I made it to Austin. There was a picture of a deteriorating skeleton in the sand with a huge "DON'T" written over the top of it and a list of twenty don'ts: Don't leave your car if it breaks down, don't go without water, don't go without food, don't this, don't that. I thought: How about don't read this poster and don't worry about it!

I headed out east on old Highway 80. Desert, sagebrush, and a whole lot of nothing in every direction. It started with a bumpy road, which jarred my body every five feet. When I stopped the bike the silence was engulfing. No cars, trains, trucks, people, birds, or wind, just pure silence.

The pleasure of the day was short-lived. I was having hot/cold flashes and a lack of energy. I could tell I was starting to get a fever. It had become obvious that breaking up with Lisa would need a considerable amount of healing. With a big storm coming and money in the budget, it was time for a hotel.

I arrived in El Centro about one o'clock and found a room in a sleazebag motel for twenty dollars. I slept all day, sweating with a fever and coughing a painful hack. I phoned Deanna that night and we had phone sex. It was my first time ever!

The first light of day and I felt worse than the day before. There were torrential rains happening outside. I had no appetite and no problem sleeping all day long, waking up for short spurts to watch *Popeye* and *Gilligan's Island*. The news warned of flooding and more rain while I took cold showers to try to break the fever. More sleep.

When I woke up it was downpouring again. How can the sky hold so much water? Another day in the motel because I still had my fever. About 9:30 in the morning the rain stopped. Maybe I will be able to ride today, I thought. I went to the store for a coffee, and some fresh air. There was a foot and a half of water in the street over the meridian, over the sidewalk, and past the lamp-post. Shit. The water was above my pedals.

The flood receded by noon. It was sixty miles to Yuma; if I packed and rode like hell I could make it by dark. I packed every-thing, the fever picked up, and I fainted back to bed. When I coughed my chest was so painful it brought tears to my eyes.

I woke up the next morning thinking only eighteen days to Deanna. It was clear and sunny with winds from the west. I phoned Channel 13 in Yuma, set up an interview for the next day and left El Centro at 9:30, making thirty-four miles in two hours. Even though my lungs ached and I had a fever, the thirty-mile-an-hour tailwinds made for a great time. It was difficult to see the road at times because of blowing sandstorms. Dust to go with that dry nagging cough.

The scenery had changed to rolling sand dunes with fences and telephone poles almost completely buried. I arrived in Yuma at 2:00 P.M., completely fatigued by the elements and the ride. Yuma attracts thousands of retired people to its warm sunny climate. Snowbirds they call 'em, and they migrate here every winter. At 8th Street RV, I asked the camp host if I could camp there. While he was check-ing, a retired couple came in to rent a spot. The lady handed the registration card to the husband for him to fill out. "Honey, what year is our RV?" the snowbird asked his wife. "Oh, that doesn't matter," said the host. "We just need a next of kin in case you 'decease' while you're here."

They had no room so I ended up at the Riverfront RV Park where Milton, Jean, and their son Mike set me up with a camp-ing spot for no charge. Before I knew it I was surrounded by 300

LOU

STOLEN
ORANGES
HERE

THIEVING LOU'S
PANTS

seniors. They had a community center where people came to play cards and other games. It sure was nice hanging out with the guys at the pool table. These guys were determined to have a blast till they kicked the bucket. I was exhausted so I jumped into the tent and crashed.

The next morning was my first TV interview for EnviroRide. The interview went well and would be on the next night, on Channel 13. After the interview I met Lou, a retired bus driver. He suggested we hop on our bikes and go for a ride to the store.

Lou asked me all kinds of questions with an ear-to-ear grin while we rode. "Have you ever grabbed oranges off trees?" he asked me with a gleam in his eye. "Not really," I said. "Well, Lou's law is, if it's over the fence, it's yours." I was stealing oranges with a senior citizen! After all that, thieving Lou and his wife, Dorothy, had me over for dinner.

It was pouring rain with flash flood warnings on the TV when I got out of the tent the next morning. As I was packing up one of the seniors showed me the newspaper. Roads closed, flooding, etc., etc. Oh well, another day in the Seniors' Ward.

Bill, one of the seniors, asked me over for dinner. Bill, his wife, another camper named Tom, and I congregated around the table. The first course: salad with "Ruby Red" salad dressing. Tom made the mistake of asking what was in it. "Well, I start with a ketchup base . . ." Ketchup, did you say ketchup? Did you do too much acid in the sixties, dude? I would rather eat a mounded spoonful of steaming mayonnaise, or drink a cup of olive oil, or toast that's been thrown into water, anything but ketchup on my salad.

TOM AND TED AFTER DINNER

I survived dinner, did laundry and Dorothy told me something exciting. Tomorrow at five-thirty in the morning, there was a bus leaving for Nevada to take people gambling. Someone was sick so I could go for free.

Dorothy was up at four in the trailer so I got up to take a shower and shave. She had coffee and cigarettes for breakfast while I had fresh fruit and juice. The bus arrived and suddenly I was experiencing yet another form of travel. One minute I was heading east on a bicycle, the next minute I was playing bingo with thirty seniors heading north to Nevada. The scenery on the three-hour trip to Laughlin was just empty desert, then this town pops up out of nowhere. Huge Las Vegas-style hotels lined the strip.

What did the Universe have in store for me today? All kinds of people hoping to make that quick buck. Plenty of pissed-off adults jockeying for greed. I gambled $5 dollars' worth of nickels then spent the rest of the afternoon walking outside taking some fun pictures with Coconut Head. I talked to one man who had lost $11,000 gambling in three days.

At 5:30 P.M. I fell asleep in the lobby of the Flamingo Hilton. I awoke to hear a woman saying, "There's no happy people." That's what it was. There were no happy people there. Take me back to the happy people. Back on the bus! Tomorrow I was riding for sure. I had only ridden three of the last eight days.

I packed up my bike and had breakfast with Lou and Dorothy. I had gotten along so well with these two, and so many others. I don't know why everybody had been so generous but I sure was enjoying it. The weather had broken a bit and I was excited about getting on the road. Dorothy had tears in her eyes as I rode away. When I was a block away they were still smiling and waving.

I BET MY CAR, HOUSE, AND WIFE AND LOST EVERYTHING. I GUESS YOU COULD CALL IT BAD LUCK

The Adventures of Coconut Head

I had a slight incline and a headwind as I crossed the border into Arizona. Highway 85 to Phoenix had been washed out, so I would just have to catch Phoenix on the next bike trip. I was more interested in making it to Aleck's in Tucson on time.

The desert was both desolate and beautiful. I enjoyed interacting with people, but I could only interact with Mother Earth while I was out in the open on a bike. I sang "Blackbird" by the Beatles to help keep my momentum up through the headwind. A lunch of peanut butter and bread as I kept heading east in search of a safe place to sleep. Just outside of Wellton I found an old orange grove that I hoped would keep me sheltered.

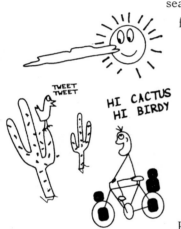

TWEET
TWEET

HI CACTUS
HI BIRDY

At 5:30 P.M. the skies opened up to continue flooding the state and forced me in my tent. Out in the desert there are a lot of flash floods. It rains so hard that the ground becomes saturated and makes instant rivers. One minute it can be a dry dusty plain, the next thing you know it's a whitewater fiesta.

I started dinner, a harmony of vegetables and pasta. My snacks simmered away as I sucked propane fumes inside my little home. It was just about done when I knocked the stove over, sending scalding water, veggies, and pasta all over me and my sleeping bag. The stove was cooking the side of the tent. Lunging for it, I knocked over the candle, sending a spray of hot wax around me as I was plunged into the dark, sitting in a pool of wax, veggies, and pasta. I could see the headlines: Frozen Biker Found Covered in Wax and Vegetables. Satanic Vegetarian Cult Suspected.

January 13. I awoke lonely in between the dead orange trees. I had been on the road for three months. Waking up to cold wax and vegetables everywhere was less than encouraging. I was glad I had a bit of money to keep me going. I still thought a lot about Lisa but I was more focused on reconnecting with Deanna. As I chowed my pancakes at the local restaurant I overheard the locals ranting and raving about the flooding. I have heard of global warming, but this was more like global raining. They all had a good laugh at me for trying to deal with the weather.

The highway continued to be a gradual uphill climb with more headwinds. I finally started to get a little hill karma. I raced down the hill, Coconut Head fell off into the deadly highway and was run over by a car. He lost part of his neck and was in a state of shock.

AND WHERE DO YOU THINK YOU ARE GOING YOUNG MAN?

TO GET RUN OVER BY A CAR?

I began to doubt my own strength while I pressed back uphill into the wind. More storms were on the way. At Mohawk there was a rest stop where I started talking to a man with a pickup truck. He offered to take me out of the danger zone. OK. I threw my bike in the back. I knew the Universe wanted me out of danger.

Bob, who was in the army, told me about how the U.S. military forces loved to smoke pot during Vietnam. I wondered if it was a good thing to have the people who protect you all smoking dope. I guess if they were like Bill Clinton and didn't inhale it was OK. He dropped me off ten miles west of Stanfield. The winds had shifted, the hill was gone.

Cranking the miles out, I stopped to see a huge feed lot that had once been owned by John Wayne. Well over 100,000 head of cattle were crammed into this tiny area. Knee deep in mud, with very little protection, these creatures were stacked up as far as the eye could see. I told them that I loved them and that one day they would be free.

The Adventures of Coconut Head

MY
STOMACH

I made it to Casa Grande with only thirty minutes of daylight left. I saw a farmhouse just out of town and knocked on the door. A woman answered, and I asked her if it was OK to camp in her yard. With a huge smile on her face she said, "No" and slammed the door in my face.

I went to the next farm. "Hi! Come on in," Betty said with a smile. "Is there room for a tent in your yard?" I asked. "Tent? How about the spare bedroom? Here's a towel for a shower, and can we take you out for Mexican food?" How sweet it was. They just wanted to help someone have a better day. It's odd that the media totally exploits violence in America yet there are so many wonderful people.

For breakfast, Betty whipped up some waffles and I was on the way again. It was over sixty miles to Tucson, mostly uphill with another headwind. There was an old frontage road that ran along I-10, making for easy, safe riding. I wanted to ride at least halfway there before I stopped for lunch.

There were very few cars on the frontage road. Wide open desert with mountains popping out of the ground like a whole bunch of noses on a flat face. After twenty miles I was starving. The town of Redrock was still ten miles away so I kept trudging on. My stomach was doing backflips when I got to Redrock. It only had a gas station and the next town was another twelve miles. At this point I was riding one mile at a time convincing myself, "You can do it, you can do it!" After about six miles I had to stop.

I got off my bike ready to faint. The ground was saturated so I lay down face up on the road. I probably looked like I had just had a heart attack, but cars went past me like they had never even seen me.

I finally made it to Cortara and ate pizza like it was the last supper. The whirly winds had kicked in and now the wind was blowing towards Tucson. I arrived at Aleck's in Tucson seventy-five miles later completely exhausted.

The next day I woke up feeling like I had been hit by a speeding freight train. The last stretch of heartbreak, loneliness, and highway had nearly destroyed me. I lay horizontal on the couch all day watching reruns of *The Simpsons* on TV.

January 17. That afternoon Aleck and I caught the matinee showing of *Alive*—the story of the rugby team whose plane crashed in the Andes. The remaining few ended up eating the dead bodies to survive. And I thought I was on a limited diet.

VIEW FROM ONE OF THE

PASSING CARS

That night I wrote up my first newsletter about the trip. My plan had been to write four issues and sell subscriptions as a means of making money on the road. There was still a week before I would get to see Deanna. I kept trying to keep the brightest, clearest memory of her at the center of my attention.

The next night there was another huge storm. I decided to approach the media when things were a little slower. A biker riding around the country doesn't mean much when a city is being burned, looted, tornadoed, flooded, or whatever. President Bush had declared the state of Arizona a disaster area. By five that afternoon I had packaged over 170 letters.

Inauguration Day, the day Bill told George to get the hell out of my Oval Office, and by the way where are the keys to the limo. Meanwhile, in world news the U.S. was still blowing the shit out of Iraq. Georgie had to kick Saddam in the shins one more time before he went on unemployment insurance.

The Adventures of Coconut Head

The next day was spent delivering press releases. I dropped into KTZN, a light rock station where Corey the afternoon jock asked me to come in and do an interview right then and there. I was unable to make all the deliveries. CBS seemed interested and said they would get back to me. Thirty-five miles later I made it back home.

Lisa had left a message on the voice mail. I hadn't heard anything from her since that teary-eyed day in San Diego. I called her later that night and it was nice to talk to her. She had gotten a job on Vancouver Island and seemed to be in good spirits. Talking to her on the phone I realized the incredible strengthening of spirit our split had created. I told her that I loved her and wished her well.

The next morning I woke up at 5:30 to shower and shave. I had agreed to speak at a local Toastmaster's club at 6:20 in the morning. After a three-mile ride in the fresh morning air, I arrived to a group of fairly dense people. My speech was about following your heart and your dreams. Most of the group fell asleep while I was speaking.

LIVE YOUR PASSION, FOLLOW YOUR HEART!

I AM TOO OLD   ZZzzz

After the meeting I rode through some of the upper-class areas of Tucson. Beautiful large homes with creative architecture, a far cry from the blatant consumerism I had experienced in Hollywood. I passed through a park where a group was huddled around a fire. It was a gathering of indigenous peoples celebrating a new year by the coming of the new moon. They fed me oatmeal while we chatted about their mission of saving sacred lands from the wrath of development.

Riley, one of the native women, performed a sacred ceremony

on me. She put cedar in an abalone shell then waved the magic smoke over my body, my bike, and Coconut Head. Riley assured me that I would finish my journey unharmed. After my magic smoke ceremony I rode back to Aleck's.

KURT GOFF

CBS-TV called my message center and wanted to do a piece. I set up a rendezvous and loaded up the bike for the cameras. Kurt Goff, the anchor from the six o'clock news, came out for the interview. He was highly impressed and made Coconut Head the center of the story. They ended up running the piece on the five, six, and ten o'clock news.

First thing the next morning Deanna called to tell me that she would be arriving late Monday night with friends who were driving her to Tucson. As I gave her the exact directions, reality was becoming more attractive. I no longer needed to depend on a memory to be with Deanna, it was the real thing.

Over three weeks of anticipation had passed for this beautiful specimen of spirit and flesh to wrap around me and today was the day that Deanna was going to arrive.

BANG

START GUN

About 3:30 in the morning she made it. Oh my God! I could tell this relationship had stretched our comfort zones. We spent an hour just talking and looking into each other's eyes, regaining that spiritual connection. We finally went to sleep sometime after five.

At 8:50 A.M. the doorbell was ringing. I had set up an interview with Ed Severson at the *Arizona Daily Star* for nine that morning. Ed was early. I woke Deanna up, "Well, honey, this is where your adventure begins!" Ed did an hour-long interview and asked very interesting questions. He focused on: What kind of person does it take to make a ride like this? What do your parents

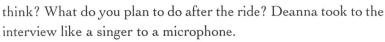

think? What do you plan to do after the ride? Deanna took to the interview like a singer to a microphone.

Deanna and I really needed a bit of time together before we could hit the highway. Aleck was nice enough to let us stay just a little bit longer. For five days straight Deanna and I talked, made love, talked, and made love. We really got back to that original level of attraction and went to the next level of intimacy. It was true love from the first moment I saw her.

After getting reconnected I felt it was important for Deanna to learn about Canada so I rented an educational video for her, *Strange Brew*. It featured two experts on Canadian culture, Bob and Doug McKenzie.

I also asked Aleck to take some new promo pictures with Deanna. We drove out into the desert to visit those big, tall cactuses. A picture here, a picture there, then we started taking naked pictures. Getting naked seemed to be a theme in our relationship. I turned a corner and almost fell off my bike stark naked into a big prickly cactus. I recovered but smashed my tailbone into the center bar of my bike. One must be careful while riding without clothes in the land of prickly giants!

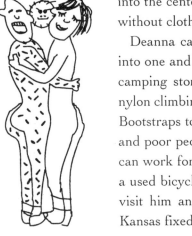

Deanna came with two brand-new sleeping bags that zipped into one and $300 so we headed out to buy some supplies at the camping store. We bought a compact stove, a tarp, and some nylon climbing strap. Aleck had a friend named Kansas who runs Bootstraps to Share. This organization builds bikes for homeless and poor people from old donated bicycles. Less fortunate folks can work for five dollars an hour credit towards the purchase of a used bicycle. A unique and heartwarming project. We went to visit him and to donate some extra bicycle pants and shorts. Kansas fixed us up with reflectors, kick stands, and bike lights.

Bootstraps to Share also builds trailers for bikes. We met a landscaper who carried all his tools around on his trailer behind his bike. Four hours later we finally got out of there. Back to Aleck's for food and a nap.

Kansas had a connection at KXCI radio so he arranged an interview for 6:45 that night. We had fifteen minutes on the air. I had so much to say that even fifteen minutes wasn't enough. "Everybody wants a better world, everybody can do something, everybody makes a difference!" The whole control room was clapping and cheering!

Three weeks in L.A. and almost three weeks in Tucson had really slowed the pace of the trip down. With Deanna here, the new stove, real sleeping bags, my heart and body healed, there was a new wave of enthusiasm for EnviroRide. It was time to get back on the road.

DEANNA WAS READY FOR CAMPING

Bring on West Texas

Tucson, Arizona, to Austin, Texas

February 2, 1993. It was sunny and warm when we bid farewell to Aleck the next morning. I had traveled almost 2,500 miles and Deanna had never been on a bike for more than two miles at a time. I was both apprehensive and curious about what was going to happen that day.

The first sixteen miles were uphill with headwinds and one of Deanna's knees was already starting to hurt. We stopped at the Saguaro National Monument for camping directions and found out that ten miles down the road at the Colossal Caves was a free campground. There were saguaro cactuses everywhere and roadrunners all over the place. I felt like I was living in a cartoon.

Dee was bouncing around on her bicycle like it was a trampoline. She had so many new things happening she wouldn't listen to my cycling suggestions. Within five miles she was completely frantic and in tears, unable to pedal her bike another inch. We still had quite a distance to go and it was completely dark. We were walking our bikes when I asked myself, Am I torturing this poor city woman? We finally made it to the park gate. She laughed, she cried, she had made it thirty miles.

The gates were all locked up so we had to lift our bikes over the fence. In the distance there was a house with lights on. Knock, knock, knock. A man came out of the house with a loaded .45 handgun. "What do you want?" he bellowed. "Hi, my name is Ted and this is Deanna. Where is the free camping?" I swiftly guessed we were at the wrong spot. Call it a hunch. He told us where the campground was as he shook his gun at us. I told Deanna that I knocked on people's doors all the time.

HAVING A GOOD TIME HONEY?

Down the hill, over the fence, off to the campground, then over the campground fence. The place was completely deserted. We set up the tent, then I massaged Deanna. She was thrilled by the idea of a massage but quickly passed out from exhaustion.

NOTHING AFFECTED DEANNA UNTIL SHE WAS INFORMED THAT THERE WERE NO SHOWERS AVAILABLE

Consider what Deanna had been through today. She had cycled thirty miles uphill into a headwind with a fully loaded bicycle. She had knee problems and had to pee in the bushes in danger of falling into a cactus. Or how about having a loaded .45 pulled on her? Now she was camping for the first time in her life. There were no showers or bathrooms. Not once did she even hint at complaining. What a woman!

It was damn cold in the tent that morning. The winds were gusting up to thirty miles an hour from the east. I didn't think Deanna would be able to ride into this breeze. Since it was free camping we stayed another day and went up to the Colossal Caves. I think caves have magic earth energy inside.

After lunch a Latino man and his family strolled by our campsite. Abundio was so excited about EnviroRide he took up a collection and gave us nineteen dollars. People in every state had poured out their love, food, and money.

GIVING IS GOOD

We tied our climbing strap in between two trees making "The Balance Game." It is just like walking a tightrope except it is only two inches off the ground. At first you can only stay on for half a second. As you practice you learn to relax, breathe, trust, and stay on longer. We were learning to be balanced.

This was the first day in Deanna's life without a shower and she was none too balanced about it. I stuck my leather wallet between her teeth so she wouldn't bite her tongue off. That night we rode into the desert to watch the sun descend behind the majestic saguaro cactuses. Back at the campground we built a huge fire illuminating our space. We made love in the center of the campground under the Arizona stars and fell asleep to the moon splashing the campground in mysterious light.

The next day it was back to the bikes: headwinds and a 1,000-foot grade to start our day. The road was up and down, up and down. I assisted Deanna with her cycling technique. On her second day of riding she discovered that her bike had gears, making the riding for this beaming bright-eyed woman a little easier.

We passed through the small town of Benson, and the first house we saw out of town we solicited for accommodations. Dean and his wife, two heavy-duty Mormons, told us we could camp in their yard and they didn't pull a gun on us. Dee was ecstatic that she had ridden forty-two miles.

They had us in for dinner while they told us about their thirteen kids and seventeen grandkids. Dean's wife had been pregnant for nine years and nine months. They were really nice people who must have played doctor every single day to have that many kids. Deanna got another massage before we drifted off to sleep.

The chickens in the yard woke us up and the bikers hit the highway. We stopped for fries before we tackled the 4,975-foot summit of Texas Canyon. The canyon looked like a 200-foot person had balanced dinosaur-sized rocks on top of stacks of Ted-sized rocks. If there were ever an earthquake they would all come tumblin' down.

The climb was a breeze and Deanna aced the whole hill. Three or four miles past the summit on I-10 was "The Thing": a tourist ordeal to attract people to the Dairy Queen. I paid the cash to see "The Thing" but I am sworn to secrecy. Even if I wanted to tell you what it was, I couldn't because "The Thing" would come get Coconut Head and my bike.

After "The Thing" we had a big ol' cruise downhill past the turnoff for Highway 666. We saw some javalinas, which kind of look like pigs. Somebody told me they *descended* from the rodent family whereas someone else said they were *part of* the rodent family. Shit, as long as they had a family that's all that matters.

I HAVE BEEN PREGNANT FOR NINE AND 3/4 YEARS. HONEST, I REALLY ENJOYED IT

YOUR AVERAGE RODENT FAMILY

For the past couple of days there had been a lot of cattle in fields beside the highway. As we passed every moo-moo, they put their cud down so they could have a gander at us. I guess they had never seen bicycles before.

We pulled into Willcox, along Business Route I-10. So many of these little towns were devastated when the Interstate and the main highway passed them by. Gas stations, motels, pubs, and bars that once had a booming business were now boarded up or just hanging on by whatever cash flow the locals could provide. I wondered why people lived in Willcox.

Another stop for fries. My intuition told me to get a hotel that night. When we got out of the restaurant there was a full-blown storm happening. By the time we got into the hotel the sky was unloading buckets of water outside. That intuition. Inside Deanna took shower after shower to catch up on the ones she had missed.

We went for breakfast at a place called the Regal. Every person that walked in was showered by hellos and how ya doings. We said a few hellos ourselves. There we met Jim who thought we were a big newspaper story, so he escorted us back to the *Arizona Range News*, which was started in 1880. Greg, the owner, had lost over 100 pounds of excess weight by cycling . . . all right Greg!

- GREG -

BEFORE CYCLING.

AFTER CYCLING.

Bring on West Texas

The afternoon whizzed by with tailwinds and an expansive stretch of riding downhill. We stopped at the San Simon truck stop for a break, exhausted and ready to call it a day. The first house we saw we pulled up to check it out. Patsy said it would be fine for us to camp in the back. Her husband, Bill, came out and told us that we could sleep in the hangar. Hangar? They had their own airplane and landing strip. Not to mention fifty pecan trees that we could help ourselves to. We set up in the hangar and shelled pecans for hours.

It was a cold dark night in the hangar with the plane. I woke up in the middle of it thinking it was morning. I cut up some oranges and pulled Deanna out of the sleeping bag. "Get up, get up," I said. She looked at me as if I were crazy. I looked at my watch. It was 3:04 A.M. Back to bed.

We left early in the pouring rain and headed back to the truck stop until the weather eased off. More tailwinds. Deanna was doing really well until we got caught in a hailstorm in the middle of nowhere. "I have never been outside in a major storm, ever!" she grieved. A thick black cloud blocked the sun. The storm was moving closer and closer. Deanna went into interrogation mode. "Where are we going to hide from big hail balls? How many big hail balls does it take to crack a bike helmet?"

Huge tumbleweeds were speeding across the highway. Luckily we only experienced the outer edge of the storm. We made it to Lordsburg, New Mexico, twenty miles east of the Arizona border tired and cranky. Both of us had credit cards and they were both maxed out. Since the grocery store didn't check them, we bought some groceries. As we walked out of the store, the skies released their fury and it started to hail big time. Within five minutes there

IT'S TIME TO WAKE UP!

DO HAIL BALLS HURT?

YOU NEVER SAID THAT WE MIGHT BE PUMMELED BY LARGE PIECES OF ICE

CAN LIGHTNING BE PAINFUL?

DEANNA

was an inch of ice on the ground. We took shelter from the storm by charging a hotel room.

There was sunshine and tailwinds in the morning. Yee-ha! We decided to take it easy and ride only thirty miles. Riding through this part of the world there was absolutely nothing but desert. The only safe place we could find to camp at was a highway rest stop. We arrived about two o'clock and the wind had an arctic bite to it. We cooked up some canned beans from the store in Lordsburg. Our lunch tasted twenty years old.

Three o'clock in the afternoon and it was too cold to read, write, or do anything. There was absolutely nothing to do but huddle up and watch the trucks go by. It was pretty exciting when a Greyhound bus went past. After that we just stayed busy keeping our food down.

Once it was dark, Deanna and I walked out into the middle of the field behind the rest stop. We gazed up into the cold, clear night. This was another Deanna first, stargazing. We saw Mars, Jupiter, the Big Dipper, and the Little Dipper. We continued walking, talking about all of our dreams and passions. Then we set up the tent, crawled into bed and froze our little butts off.

Dee's tire had a flat when we got up the next morning and when I tried to fix it I broke the valve. Stranded in the middle of nowhere, we needed a ride. Richard, a Canadian war veteran, drove us into Las Cruces. On the way, he told us stories about how during the Second World War, Canadian soldiers suffered more injuries from drunken cycling accidents than from Germans.

We spent the night in Las Cruces after getting Dee's bike fixed and left early the next morning. Our first stop was Anthony,

Texas, the first town across the New Mexico/Texas border. Everybody waved there. People were running out of their Mexican-style adobe homes, dogs, tow truck drivers, everyone waved. I felt like the Queen.

We stopped at a store where we met Robert, who was most interested in our ride. He told us that El Paso, which was next on our route, was "fumongous." I asked him if that meant fucking humongous. He said it just meant really big, then he told us he was a minister. Oopsie.

We made it to El Paso after a forty-five-mile ride. Lloyd and Jean, friends of Deanna, still lived another fifteen miles away. It was almost dark as we rode through town. Across the road was the Rio Grande River and the slum town of Ciudad Juárez. Hundreds, if not thousands of people were crammed into tiny cardboard homes and metal shacks.

On one side of the river, restaurants, hotels, fancy homes, and nice cars. On the other side sick babies, no sewage system, and no doughnut stores. How could anybody walk by here and not be frustrated? The people on the Mexican side were starving to death while people on the American were deciding if they should do another round at the buffet.

ROBERT's TRUE IDENTITY

ONE GUY'S HOUSE   ONE HOUSE FOR ALL THESE GUYS

BUFFET

U.S.A.

MEXICO

The Adventures of Coconut Head

By the time we got to Lloyd and Jean's, Deanna was very excited that she had set her own mileage record of sixty miles. Jean had this overwhelming need to do something. Do you want to see the house, how about some pictures, cards, Trivial Pursuit, read, go to the movies? After seven hours of riding Dee and I had a severe case of Confused Biker Syndrome and were unable to handle the situation so we pretended to fall asleep.

I BLAME THE GOVERNMENT FOR EVERYTHING THAT IS BAD

We started the next day with strong west winds while heading south on Highway 20. The scenery was still 100 percent desert in every direction. We rode until we arrived in Fort Hancock. A huge tumbleweed five feet in diameter crossed our path as we pulled into the coffee shop. Inside the local political critics were hard at work. The group agreed that as soon as they figured out what the problems were they would have all the political solutions.

We went back on the road through the desert, making a total of seventy miles by day's end. A truck stop had some space in the back for us to have a fire and camp. Another starry night and free camping.

A 1,500-foot climb for breakfast, with a side order of headwinds. West Texas had miles and miles of nothingness. We continued on to Van Horn looking for a place to camp. A motel seemed to be a better option because we both stank. All we needed was a hotel that didn't have a credit card checker thing. We found the Country Inn Motel and our host Lorraine. Once we got in the room we kicked back admiring the cowboy boots on the walls stuffed with dried flowers.

The next day I woke up with zero energy. We hadn't had more than a day off since Tucson. Physically, my body was saying, "Chill dude, chill." OK, I'll chill. We watched TV and wrote letters for most of the day.

Lorraine phoned the next morning at 7:00 A.M. and told us it was only 19°F outside with a strong arctic wind from the east. Another day of rest in the hotel.

The tailwind was gusting "fumongously" the next day and we made thirty miles by noon, finding a gully for shelter and lunch. The wind was blowing so hard it was impossible to ride any other direction except east, which happened to be the direction we were going. Coasting at thirty miles an hour, with a downhill top speed of forty-four.

February 17. We had covered 576 miles that month. Eight hours of exciting riding and desolate desert later we were in Balmorrhea. We had only three dollars until we hit a bank machine, which was still at least fifty miles away.

THE WIND IS OUR FRIEND!

Balmorrhea was a very cool town. I could tell it was very friendly by the dogs. Riding around, the dogs came out to play or just look. I feel that dogs are a reflection of their owners. Mean dogs, mean owners. But, does the same apply to roosters? We met Shawn, a young Mexican man, who had fighting roosters. Shawn told us how he tied blades to the birds' claws so they could kill each other more easily. Just how friendly is that? Two doors down we found a house that looked friendly. Knock, knock. "Sure you can stay, but we're having a funeral first thing in the morning," Wes said.

Fighting roosters like to cock-a-doodle-doo all night long. Maybe that's why they try to kill each other. After having no sleep myself, those roosters could kill each other as far as I was concerned. The next morning Wes had us in for breakfast with his family. On the way out, Wes was emptying his canned tuna fish out of the pantry and his money out of his wallet for us. We thanked him and wished him a happy funeral.

After this pleasant interlude we were back on the highway. I had been looking at this desert for the past 1,200 miles. The only scenery that really changed was the road kill. I was going mental. Sixty miles later we made it to Fort Stockton for a money machine. We went another twenty-five miles watching a beautiful sunset as Mother Nature blasted us towards Austin. We camped right beside an exit ramp and crawled five feet into a drainage tunnel to get shelter from the wind. When was the last time you cooked dinner in a drainage tunnel? That was a record day: eighty-five miles.

It was only eighty-seven miles to the next town, Ozona. No headwinds, no problem. Deanna was doing a fantastic job. Her performance level was much higher than I had expected. We started early at a smooth pace. It was hot and dry out on the tarmac. Through this part of the desert we saw only one or two gas stations a day. When we did see one, we filled our six water bottles plus an extra one-gallon container. After sixty miles we were completely out of water, without a source in sight. It was dead still through that beige desolate part of the planet, except for the squawk of vultures in the distance. We had to make the extra miles. We ate every piece of fruit we had to keep our fluid levels up.

Eighty-seven miles: a new record and a new level of exhaustion. With only four days of riding to Austin, Florida was getting just a little closer. Worn out, we checked into the closest non-Mastercard checking hotel.

The brown landscape slowly rolled by in the breeze of the open desert. After sixty miles we pulled off the Interstate to set up the tent. We had to sleep in the ditch because the endless nothingness was fenced off. We didn't want to be mistaken for trespassers.

As I stood outside the tent the next morning letting the desert air fill my sinuses I thought about Deanna and how her physical stamina had improved by leaps and bounds. We had cycled 245 miles in three days and Dee's greatest concern was if she was considered an athlete yet.

WHAT ARE YOU DOING?

It was cool when we got out of the tent but the sun gently pushed the thermometer up, up, and away. Midway up a long hill I got a flat tire. I tried pumping it up, but it immediately went flat again. I felt physically exhausted—the heat, the mileage, the flat—the whole deal pushed me over the edge. Dwayne pulled up in his pickup truck and kindly offered the use of his compressor from his house. By the time we finished walking up the hill to Dwayne's house, I was completely mental.

I'M LEAPING AND BOUNDING

We asked Dwayne if we could camp in his yard. He said yes with a little resistance in his voice. His resistance seemed odd until we met his wife. She was the coldest, anger-shootingest lady in West Texas. Deanna thought the guy who pulled the gun on us was more friendly than Dwayne's wife.

We spent the night camping at 666 Satan Street but left without saying good-bye and stopped at a truck stop about eight miles down the road for breakfast. Half a mile away from the truck stop my tire went flat again. Seven patches and two hours later we were back on the highway with only twelve miles to the 290 turnoff.

Twelve miles didn't seem far until a bad-tempered headwind started manipulating our game plan. We were blown to a dead stop twice. It was impossible to ride more than a half mile at a time. I feared collapsing, and being stranded in the middle of nowhere.

ARE YOU STILL OUR FRIEND MR. WIND?

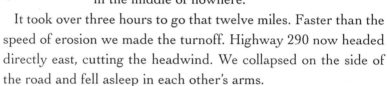

It took over three hours to go that twelve miles. Faster than the speed of erosion we made the turnoff. Highway 290 now headed directly east, cutting the headwind. We collapsed on the side of the road and fell asleep in each other's arms.

We woke up half an hour later and Deanna said, "I would rather have needles stuck in my nose than have to do that again." I agreed. We finally made it to the town of Harper, Texas. Knock, knock. "Can we stay in your yard?" "Sure you can stay, my name is Julian and this is my son Julian. Would you rather stay in the spare room? There's a tornado watch this evening," the man said. Thank God and thank Julian too, beds to sleep in. We sat down for coffee with his mom, dad, and eight-year-old niece Priscilla.

**THIS
IS NOT
THAT
PAINFUL**

DEANNA

Mom and Dad were in their seventies and spoke no English. Since I knew no Spanish, Julian translated for us. I brought in some pictures of the trip to share with the gang but I didn't realize that silly pictures spoke all languages. Mom and Dad laughed and laughed at the pictures of us butt naked in the desert. I fell asleep in a state of bliss once again.

In the morning they made us eggs and toast. These people with so little had such huge hearts. Whatever they could offer to make our life more enjoyable, they wanted us to have it. I was learning one of the most enriching parts of life: the gift of giving unconditionally with no expectations of a payback.

We had planned to be in Austin the following night and had peddled our little butts off to make it for *The Simpsons* on TV. But by 6:00 P.M. we were still fifty miles from Austin. Six miles past Johnson City we were attacked by four little chihuahuas looking for some leg. Small dogs make great footballs if they get close enough.

A mile later we found a farmhouse. We pulled in and were surrounded by thirteen more frantic chihuahuas. A young lad named Buddy holding a .22 rifle came out to calm the frothing-at-the-mouth puppies. "Don't shoot, don't shoot," Deanna screamed to the armed farmer. He went to ask his Granny if we could stay. Gramma showered us with fresh homemade doughnuts and coffee cake and Buddy showed us where to set up the tent.

"Y'all wanna watch TV out here?" Buddy asked. He set the television up, under the carport. I couldn't believe I was watching the Simpsons while I was camping. Homer and Bart did their thing while we were surrounded by thirteen dogs, four cats, three baby sheep, and an eighteen-year-old redneck.

THIS IS A WEIRD CAMPING EXPERIENCE

YES DEAR

Buddy showed me his loaded .45, which he kept by his side. Why would an eighteen-year-old kid need to carry a loaded .45 handgun? We jumped into the tent that night, completely excited that neither of us carried loaded .45s. We must have said "I love you" to each other a hundred times.

I had a dream that Princess Diana and Prince Chuck wrote me a letter. They said they were putting in their two weeks' notice with London because Monaco had offered them a job. Monaco had $450 trillion in the royal fund, and the letter guaranteed me that once the royals got their expense accounts, they would be able to kick in a generous donation to EnviroRide.

The morning sun was blocked by the shadows of little baby sheep on the side of the tent. West Texas had nearly put us both over the edge. This was our eighth day of straight riding and we were both fairly wacko. We met up with Buddy in the house and he showed us what was boiling in a pot on the back burner—the bunny he had shot last night. We departed while Buddy shot at the birds in the yard with his .22. Bye-bye gun boy.

We stopped for a break at a grocery store where I purchased a six-pack of cookies. Deanna and I bought treats all the time. Sometimes I ate more, sometimes she did. This time I took four cookies, leaving two for Deanna, then I headed for the bathroom. She yelled at me from the opposite side of the convenience store, "Hey, how come you took one of my cookies? What gives you the right? You were going to hide in the bathroom and eat that other cookie, weren't you?"

Everybody in the store stared at us in silence while Deanna ran over to me. With a vengeance she grabbed the cookie from my hands. Crumbs flew everywhere and her eyes were filled with tears. I surrendered the "Extra Cookie" to Deanna. Had she gone totally mental with anguishaphobia?

We finally made it to Austin about four that afternoon. Deanna's friends Beverly and Duane were away for the weekend so we had their house all to ourselves. We needed it. We had cycled over 900 miles in just twenty-two days. Massive Confused Biker Syndrome had set in; simple conversation was impossible; our bodies were on the verge of collapse. This was the most physical activity mine had seen since arriving on this planet.

WEST TEXAS WAS RESPONSIBLE
FOR THE WAY WE LOOKED

Just Who Invented Headwinds, Anyway?

Austin, Texas, to Mobile, Alabama

Monday, March 1, 1993. Total distance traveled: 3,402 miles. We rested and did all those petty little chores, like laundry and refilling our bodies with copious amounts of calories. It took three full days before either of us felt human. Deanna showered and showered.

Of all the adversity we had experienced, there was only one thing that really stood out for Dee. Was it the headwinds, hailstorms, guns, lousy food, the hard ground, the complete change of lifestyle from being an intensive care nurse? No. It was the fact that she had to go five days without a shower.

Thursday, March 4. We were up at 5:30 A.M. to get ready for our first Texas radio interview. One of the first questions Allan, the morning show host, asked Deanna was, "What's a babe like you doing with such an ugly guy?" I really wanted to use the airtime for encouraging people to ride, not to broadcast Allan's perception of my physical beauty.

Just Who Invented Headwinds, Anyway?

The next morning Deanna and I went for a walk around town. We were having so much fun visiting with each other that I popped "The Question." "Do you want to get married in Key West?" I suddenly asked as we stopped at a traffic light. I had no idea where that question came from. I had had absolutely no previous thoughts about marriage to Deanna or anybody else. It popped out of my mouth like a jack-in-the-box. Dee said, "OK!" Now we were getting married.

WANT TO GET MARRIED?

WHY DID I SAY THAT?

We phoned all our friends and told them the news about our marriage plans. Everybody was very excited and so were we. I hardly slept because I was part of a "whirlwind romance!"

We woke at 5:30 A.M. for an interview with KGSR. Kevin, the host, was amazed by the whole story. At the end of the interview he looked us straight in the eye and asked, "Why are you people so damn happy?" I don't even remember what we answered. I took it as an incredible compliment that our most outstanding feature was our happiness.

We spent the rest of the day kicking back and relaxing in the sun. Austin was a very cool city, a large urban area with that small town feeling, very awake, very concerned about the betterment of the human race.

We finally got out of Austin ten days after we got there. Energized and eager to get to Florida we jumped back on our bikes into the Texas sun. The day was very hot, 85°F with 100 percent humidity.

KICKING BACK

OW, OW!

I wanted to test the "trust" theory. We mailed our timepieces, bike computer, and maps to Deanna's mom in Florida. I was curious to see how much value these methods of measurement really had. We may not know where we were exactly, or what time it was, but I had to trust that it would be OK.

The Adventures of Coconut Head

WHY ALL
THE
EXPLOSIVES?

I HAVE NO
EXPLANATION

Just past noon we saw a building with the word "fireworks" on it. When I asked if I could purchase some of them, Ralph said, "No, because we are not allowed to sell them until June 26." He asked us many questions about what we were doing so we showed him a naked desert photo. He smiled and told us to wait in the parking lot. Ralph presented us with two shopping bags full of fireworks. Explosive gifts for the happy couple.

By the time we loaded our bicycles, every single one of our bags was brimming over the top. "If a cop pulls you over just say you've been carrying them since Christmas," Ralph said. Sure. What cop is going to believe that. "Yes, I left with some clothes, a bike, and a couple hundred dollars' worth of explosives."

We camped on the side of the road in a wooded area that night. Next morning carrying twenty pounds of firecrackers didn't make battling the headwinds any easier. We struggled on to La Grange and stopped at the newspaper to tell them about EnviroRide. You know it's a small town when the editor is out delivering newspapers. The wind was howling by now and we had no energy left. Something about those headwinds just psyched us right out.

After struggling with the wind all day I really needed to get rid of all those damn firecrackers. Just east of Hempston we found Rae's house, a colorful farm with cows, geese, dogs, chickens, roosters, and Penny the wiener dog. Rae allowed us to camp on his property and blow all the explosive stuff up.

I grabbed a short fat stumpy one and set it up on a plank. I lit the sucker and ran. That rocket chased me like a cruise missile.

ROCKETS ARE
FASTER THAN ME!

I AM GOING TO
GET YOU!

Just Who Invented Headwinds, Anyway?

A fireball was coming right for my face. I hit the dirt, landing face first just inches from a cow pie.

After a thirty-minute fireworks show with whistles, smoke, and sparks we started cooking dinner. As I looked over the duck pond there was a mammoth electrical storm moving in from the west. Great, more free fireworks. Ripper bolts stretched from one end of the sky to the other. Every couple of seconds the darkness would vanish into screaming white light. I love lightning storms. Dee on the other hand completely freaked out. "Does lightning like tents? Will we die? If it actually does strike the tent do we have any chance of surviving? Is there hope?"

THERE IS NO DANGER AT ALL DEANNA

Dinner had just finished cooking when we were forced to dive into the tent. It had started hailing, which didn't bother me, but a tent isn't the safest place to be in a hailstorm. I looked outside and the hailstones were as big as jawbreakers. Dee was beginning to panic. The hail was getting more intense. The only shelter was about 100 yards away. I told Dee to wear her bike helmet if we did have to make a break for it. That calmed her down considerably. The tent held up well and I fell asleep feeling comfortable and relaxed. I can't speak for Dee though. The storm continued through the night.

The wind blew, the rain fell, the temperature dropped, the tent flooded, and the bikers froze. Everything we had was soaked. We used to have two sets of warm clothing but we'd left one in Austin because we thought it was spring. The temperature set a record low that night. Riding on the highway with a brisk, arctic crosswind, the dampness of my clothing was taking its toll. I know the signs of hypothermia. I was experiencing them.

We trudged on and made it to the outskirts of Houston. We phoned my friends Les and Kathy from a Denny's. As we cycled through an intersection on the way to their house, my rear axle snapped, making me a sitting duck for eight lanes of traffic. Oh that ol' Universe likes to test my little ass. Les had to come pick us up and take us home. We just kicked back the rest of the day trying to warm up.

IT WAS SO COLD OUT THAT BOB BACILLUS PLAYED HOCKEY INSIDE MY BIKE BAG

The morning headlines read, "Storm of the Century"; 171 people had died in the storm that had put the whole east coast of North America into a total deep freeze. I am sure glad we weren't a part of that statistic.

The next day another friend, Tom, came over in his Mazda RX-7 convertible to take my wheel in to fix the broken axle. I hopped in the ragtop, plugged in the Led Zep CD and headed out into the heart of Houston.

We played some Frisbee in front of the waterfall at the Transco Tower, then I saw downtown Houston, U of H, the Medical District, and Flower Street. For such a big city the air and streets were clean and the people friendly. Then back to the bike shop for the wheel, which cost $11. Tom took me out for pizza and bought a newsletter subscription.

Kathy, Les, Dee, and I headed south of Houston to see Les's father's yacht. Two bedrooms, two bathrooms, TV, stereo, washer, dryer, and microwave. That night we all danced around on the yacht listening to funky Caribbean music. Only two nights before I was hiding in a tent from hail and lightning and now I was living on a yacht.

It was 1:30 P.M. the next day before we actually got on the road again. Houston was huge, taking forever to get out of. I became hot and sweaty in the process. We went through the low-income district where the guns and crime were yet people were very friendly there. They all waved and offered to share their bottles of party juice. I guess they could relate to our somewhat homeless situation.

We took a frontage road about thirty miles out of town. Daryl and Geraldine let us camp in the yard. Deanna was addicted to cleanliness. She used the garden hose as a shower. It was only 40°F outside, and the water was even colder. Hiding in the dark, washing her hair. I couldn't believe it.

I usually wake up to the sound of the birds or the fresh morning sun. Today was trucks and exhaust from the Interstate beside us. Winnie was the first town we saw. At the grocery store we were approached by a couple of men in suits. After we told them where we were going, all they could say was, "Gaw Damn and Shiyit!"

We met up with Bryan the editor at the *Hometown Press*. He asked some excellent questions. It was very different from being insulted and called ugly. We gave him an autographed naked picture for his efforts. We

GAW DAMN
TRANSLATION: **NEAT**

SHIYIT
TRANSLATION: **REALLY?**

kept going east, ending up at Kermit's house, a retired Cajun Texan. Kermit had never camped in his life and was quite amazed at our adventure. He thought that all the snakes in the world were waiting to get him and that if he ever went camping he'd be done for.

We were up at 6:15 A.M. and were on the road by eight with more headwinds. We rode single file breaking the wind and alternating the lead.

Three hours and twenty-four miles later we were in the quaint little town of Port Arthur. The skyline consisted of a whack of oil refineries. As I admired the beauty of the belching smokestacks, a snake slithered past us and I thought of Kermit. Oh boy, something else to look out for. The poisonous snakes had come out of hibernation. This town made quite a little contrast for the happy environmental bikers.

Port Arthur was as friendly as a concentration camp. People would scream by in their vehicles yelling obscenities and swerving towards us. Everything about this town was less than delightful. The feeling was intensified when we crossed the Martin Luther King Jr. Bridge, which was steep, narrow, and extremely dangerous. A huge truck nearly puréed us into the guardrail. Dee lapsed into a case of I-nearly-got-run-over-by-a-truck syndrome.

A SAMPLE TOXIC FISH

It was only six miles to the Louisiana border. We had been in Texas for a long long time. Along the road there were all kinds of people fishing out of the river. Just on the other side of the river was a bunch of refineries. Now there's a fish I would never eat.

We made it across the bridge into Louisiana, a new state. God it felt great. The traffic had dwindled to a trickle but there was something new to contend with: colossal anthills crawling with big nasty red ants on both sides of the highway. Falling headfirst into one of those suckers would be ungood.

There was lush green swamp as far as our eyes could see. Birds were everywhere, teals, mallards, loons, and these big tall white egrets. It had always been an option for us to just stop on the side of the road to camp. The only place we could camp around here was on the anthills or in the water.

Everybody waved to us as we rode down the highway. We found Johnson Bayou, a quaint little town with beautiful luxurious homes. I had been expecting to see little shacks and people eating black-eyed peas. Too much Bugs Bunny as a child can warp one's perception of the world.

BUGS BUNNY

We arrived at a big house at five to seven. "Can we camp in your yard?" Since it was Thursday I had one more question to ask. "Can we watch *The Simpsons*?" "Come on in!" Faye said. When's the last time you remember strangers coming up to your house to see if they could watch TV? We ate pasta for the third night in a row and the sounds of the swamp sang us to sleep.

We left at 7:30 that morning with more headwinds. There was a mental breakdown taking place for me. This constant unrelenting, in-my-face challenge. It took almost three hours to go the twelve miles to Holly Beach.

We stopped for fries and a coffee. All this time you have probably been wondering about my fascination with French fries. Restaurants offer many things, including shelter from the wind, heating/air conditioning, rest rooms, free water, and a chance to sit on something that is butt friendly. We purchased French fries so we could take advantage of all the benefits.

The next stretch of highway ran right along the shore, which meant a higher wind speed. The waters of the Gulf of Mexico along the Louisiana coast were yucky brown. There was more junk on this beach than your average garbage dump. Plastic, washers, dryers, couches, bottles, old fishnets. By the looks of it, the good folks of Louisiana didn't give a shit about their beaches.

On the left there was a big grazing field. When we rode by, the cows thought we were rounding them up. About 150 head of cattle congregated and were moving at the same speed and in the same direction as we were. We began actually herding cows. If there were any lagging behind, some of the other cows would stop to moo at the slow-pokes encouraging them to get the lead out. We even did a couple of yee-has and as we did they would increase the pace. Half a mile later they all stopped at the fence separating them from the next field. Then out of the corner of their eye I could see the doubt. They knew we weren't real cowboys because of the smooth fluid motion of our horses.

WE KNEW YOU WERE FAKE, WE WERE JUST PLAYING

Six miles after Holly Beach we both went mental. I stopped talking and Dee couldn't stop blabbing. I did random drive-by anthill kickings. The road turned north leading us to the ferry to Cameron. Half a mile past the ferry I couldn't take any more headwinds. I had lost my sanity.

We got a room at the Gulf Motel from Murphy, the manager. We were dead beat tired as we collapsed onto the mattress.

ME

INCOMING

A look outside the window the next morning let us know that the headwinds were even stronger. We took a full day off because Murphy didn't have a credit card checker thing. Alvin moved in next door to us. He brought us a six-pack of beer and some ice cream. What a nice man.

Just Who Invented Headwinds, Anyway?

We woke up to yet another day of headwinds. Will they last the whole trip? Why are they so strong? Should we pool our cash and buy a car? Murphy stuck a couple of sandwiches in our bags and we departed into the unrelenting Louisiana breezes.

Creole was thirteen miles away, where we would head north to go to Holmwood. The wind, not wanting to feel left out, also shifted directions so that the headwinds continued to defy us. The local sheriff told us that March was official wind month for this state. I thought that after the emptiness and hilly roads of West Texas, the ride would be considerably easier. Not!

Twenty-three miles of battling headwinds with swamp to the left and right and people fishing all along the way. All the friendly faces of Louisiana had disappeared. Now there were just angry pissed-off adults. The road had no shoulder, making it difficult for cyclists and cars alike. One gentleman gave us the finger.

We stopped at a bridge to take a look at the swamp. It was eerie looking: cypress trees surrounded by water, birds, and invisible alligators.

In Hayes, we found Harrises Restaurant. The whole establishment was full of life; every table was talking, laughing, and sharing. We had found the local happy people. We ordered a crawfish sandwich. A crawfish kind of looks like a cross between a shrimp and a teeny tiny lobster. It tasted fantastic.

A couple of blocks past the restaurant we meet the Breauxes: Lawrence, Bonnie, and their two kids, Jessica and Ricky. "Can we camp in your yard tonight?" "Would you rather sleep in our new travel trailer, equipped with shower, TV, and stereo?" Lawrence inquired. "Well, OK." We visited with them for hours on the front porch. A real spacy family. Bright clear-eyed people with gentle, loving children.

IT
WILL
BE
WINDY
4-EVER

The Adventures of Coconut Head

The family was gone in the morning, but Bonnie had left us a basketful of fruit for breakfast. In Lake Arthur, the next town, our eyes popped out of our heads. They had a produce store. Finally fresh fruits and vegetables.

A few miles down the road was Gueydan (Gay dan). Mike the assistant police chief gave us police patches making us honorable constables of Gueydan, Duck Capital of America. The local newspaper did a story and we were back on the road again.

Just east of Kaplan, the next town, we met David and Doug, two Cajun brothers who had back problems and were living on welfare. They lived in one of those swamp shacks with the rocking chairs on the front porch. They couldn't believe I had ridden my bike from Canada. David said he had planned to drive there once but thought it was too damn far.

Doug's wife Mamee cooked us up some real Cajun gumbo. Then Doug told us about his neighbor's daughter who was eaten by a twelve-foot gator. They went hunting for the gator and shot him through the head. They had the pictures to prove it. It is typical of the residents of this area to eat frogs, snakes, turtle, and even gator. David told us that their brother was shot and killed while hunting. I guess somebody mistook him for a gator that could walk on his hind legs.

HI EVERYBODY

DOUG

DAVID

I WAS GOING TO DRIVE TO CANADA.. TO CANADA.. TO CANADA.. TO CANADA..

David had the wonderful personality disorder of repeating himself. The more beers he drank the more frequently he repeated the story. After the "I was going to Canada" story was told twenty-two times Dee and I called it a night, a night.

We had a quick departure the next morning to get away from David, the human broken record. In New Iberia, we finally had a tailwind. We rode the rest of the afternoon and there was a huge white plantation home on the left. Why not stay there? Sure it was a mansion, but you never knew till you asked. Karen was happy to let us stay in the yard.

Five acres with huge old oak trees, beside the Tesh Bayou. Two alligators lived in the water and Karen was concerned that her little dog Wolfgang would be eaten by them. Wolfgang hung out with us while we cooked dinner listening to the symphony of frogs and crickets in the swamp. Just before we went to bed Wolfgang humped all our bike bags for us.

WOLFGANG WAS FRIENDLY WITH THE BIKE BAGS

Sometime during the night, hundreds of teeny tiny snails crawled up and covered the tent. Dee woke up to Escargot Trauma. That day it was warm enough to ride with my shirt off. After months of riding east I have gotten an excellent tan on the right side of my body. A little strategic sunblock application and the southerly direction would start to even my tan out.

We got back onto 90 at Pattersen to phone Deanna's Aunt Judy and Uncle Bob, where we would be staying in New Orleans. The headwinds had started to blow again. These breezes had taken their toll on us. We sat outside a Walmart just wishing they would go away. While we were inside the skies opened up for a massive downpour. We sat there for an hour hoping it, like the headwinds, would also go away. It didn't so we slapped on the raingear and headed out.

HI
EVERYBODY

On 90 we had to cross some very, very, narrow bridges. The lane was only eight feet wide and gosh, that's how wide the trucks were. The semi trucks came within inches of us. It was really scary but what could I do? Change my shorts and get on with it.

The Adventures of Coconut Head

IT SMELLS LIKE FERTILIZER

THAT'S JUST MY PANTS

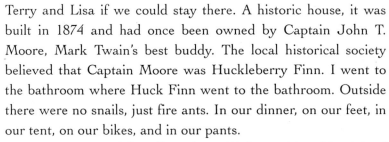

WIENERS

A few miles down the road, there was swampland on both sides of us. Riding in the rain is actually a lot of fun, when it's warm out. It rained for four hours.

About five we made it to Schreyver. There was another huge house on the left of the road and Deanna asked Terry and Lisa if we could stay there. A historic house, it was built in 1874 and had once been owned by Captain John T. Moore, Mark Twain's best buddy. The local historical society believed that Captain Moore was Huckleberry Finn. I went to the bathroom where Huck Finn went to the bathroom. Outside there were no snails, just fire ants. In our dinner, on our feet, in our tent, on our bikes, and in our pants.

Next morning while riding along Highway 90, a big slab of metal shredded my front tire. I put my thumb out, and the first truck stopped. Vu loaded the bikes up in the back of his truck and took us to the hardware store. He then chauffeured us to his home in Paradis to grab tools to change the tire. Vu was like a saint on wheels. Spreading his love and skills to keep the world moving.

Onto I-310 over the Mississippi River we passed more beautiful swampland then into the city of New Orleans to Judy and Bob's. I tried for two days solid to get media interviews but had no success.

March 27, 1993. We cooked breakfast for Judy and Bob's family, said good-bye and headed out to see the city. On Metarie Avenue was a very old cemetery. Since New Orleans is so close to sea level, the caskets are encased in cement above ground. Then they are made into huge mausoleums, some as high as twenty feet tall, complete with statues and stained-glass windows. We couldn't resist the opportunity to take a naked picture. You have to be quick to get naked pictures. You set the camera up on the tripod, get butt naked, run to the spot, and wait for the shutter. It takes only ten seconds but it seems like ten minutes before the shutter clicks.

We got unnaked and saw another photo opportunity. I set up the tripod while Deanna balanced the bikes. "Ted, come here right now, I mean now, hurry, right now," Dee wailed with tears in her eyes. I ran back. Deanna whipped her shorts off in a frenzy. "What's the matter, you got ants in your pants?" "Yes!" she screamed. When we had taken the last naked picture Deanna had thrown her shorts on an anthill. The ants had bitten her flower arrangement.

On to the French quarter in New Orleans. Artists, psychics, street performers, and hot dogs. Horse-drawn carriages weaved down the narrow streets. The old beautiful buildings whispered their colorful pasts to me. Dixieland bands played up and down the streets with all kinds of people boogying behind them.

Lunch, then we tried heading out of town. The only way to tell which direction we were going was by the direction of the sun. The sun directed us right into a rough-looking neighborhood when I stopped for directions. Two officers of the law laughed heartily in our faces because we were heading into "the projects." The cops sent us a mile back down the road to get back onto Highway 90.

After a couple of hours we were ready to call it a day. There were lake cottages on both sides of the Chef Menteur Highway when we stopped in Lake Catherine. We found a home and asked if we could stay. Delores showed us where to tent. Adam, who lived next door, said we could use his bathroom. Then Bruce and Joanne from the next house offered showers and anything else we needed. Delores came out with two cups of hot soup. Then Karl and Diane, who live on the other side, invited us in for refreshments.

It had been a while since we had heard bike horror stories. Karl told us how a biker that once stayed with him was snagged and dragged by a passing motorhome. Why do people tell us these stories?

We cooked dinner and Karl and Diane offered us a place to sleep indoors. Ever since we'd arrived here all the neighbors have been competing to see who could be the most hospitable. Karl and Diane had won! Sleeping indoors sounded absolutely marvelous. Then they took us for beer and raw oysters. Raw oysters looked like oversized amoebas that chewed like water balloons and gave me indigestion.

Sunday, March 28. We had made almost 650 miles that month. The next morning we headed out to that old highway into more fresh headwinds. The latest challenge besides the headwinds was the damn gnats. Gnats, or no-see-ums, are about a sixteenth of an inch long. Their only purpose in life is to bite or eat human flesh. After they bite, the irritation can last four or five days. They especially love necks and behind ears. I had hundreds of these little bites all over my body. I say gnot to gnats.

In Louisiana, the standard practice is to dump your trash, appliances, and old furniture onto the side of the highway or in the swamp. It's the only state where you can pull up on the side of the road, grab a beer out of the fridge, and sit on the couch.

Just Who Invented Headwinds, Anyway?

Oh, and did I mention the humidity causes you to sweat your mass off? Just another day in paradise. We crossed the border into Mississippi and camped just west of Gulfport.

The next morning we did some breathing exercises on the beautiful white sand beaches of Gulfport and absorbed all the fresh air and sunshine that was available. A man from Chicago walked up and inquired about the ride. We sold him a newsletter subscription and got that twenty in pocket. In order for the trip to continue we needed those daily donations.

About five we scoped a spot to camp near Biloxi. Gord, a fridge fixer, joined us in his backyard while we set up the tent. The conversation went something like this. "A beautiful backyard you have here." "It's OK, but the damn humidity." Change the subject. "The beaches we saw today were beautiful." "They suck, they're all man-made." Sneakily I changed the subject again. "The new gambling halls should really bring in some new business for the area." "Bastards crush the little man. I know a man who was rich, spent everything he owns. Can't afford to boil a possum now. Those damn bastards." Goodnight Gordie Gloom.

About fifteen miles down the road we crossed the Alabama line. We figured that standing naked right on the side of Highway 90 by the big "Welcome to Alabama" sign would make a great picture. It seemed like every naked picture got a little more challenging. We set the timer and dropped our drawers. It took four different attempts because of the cars passing on the road. I wonder how we would have been treated by the police of the Bible Belt for being necked in public.

The Adventures of Coconut Head

I FEEL
UNBRAVE

DEE

We arrived in Mobile, Alabama, about noon. I was unable to handle another peanut butter sandwich. Peanut butter is cheap but having it for lunch every day can drive you nuts. On the left side there was a little oriental restaurant with a buffet. While we chewed our moo gu gai pan, the skies opened up outside. Within thirty minutes there was ten inches of water in the parking lot. We laughed watching the businessmen tiptoe through the ankle-deep water to get to their cars. Ten cups of coffee later the storm finally stopped.

We were heading east on Government Street when the storm picked up again. We were already cycling in the left lane because the right lane was completely underwater. We found some shelter at a drive-through cleaners. It was now impossible to ride our bikes on the street. We had only five dollars and no contacts in Mobile. There was a hotel only six blocks away. Maybe they wouldn't check our charge card. Deanna wanted to wait for the storm to stop, but I would rather be dry in a hotel room than wet at a drycleaners. Dee still wasn't quite used to being outside in these big storms.

I AM BIKER
HEAR ME ROAR

After some encouragement we started our six-block journey. The roads were now totally under water. The first two blocks we rode on the sidewalk, yet there was still six to eight inches of water. I carried those 100-pound bikes across the second street through ten inches of water. I also carried them across the third street. By the time we got to the fourth street there were cars stalled everywhere.

Screw carrying the bikes, I decided, we would be lucky if we made it to the hotel. "BANG!" Lightning struck less than twenty-five feet away. Dee was completely freaked out, white as a ghost and out of daylights. I took control of the situation and demanded she continue. Crossing the fifth street the raging water was now over the top of my front bags. I lost and regained my balance without getting washed away. The street actually had whitewater. Why do I have a bicycle to cross a river?

The hotel was only one block away. We were walking aquariums. When we finally arrived and our credit card was refused, the manager was neither friendly nor interested in our dilemma. The only way she would help us was if hell froze over. I told her that I would watch the weather report.

Then Gail, one of the staff members, whipped out her checkbook and said, "This one is on me!" Well, thank you! We pulled every single thing out of our bags. Water poured out of my walkman and my cassettes. It had rained four inches in three hours.

People as Friendly
as Pitbulls with Rabies

Mobile, Alabama, to Key West, Florida

April Fool's Day, 1993. Total distance traveled: 4,086 miles: That storm was no joke, it really beat the purgatory out of us. The *Mobile Press* did an interview with us and we made it out of Mobile alive. After twenty-five miles we were exhausted. David lived right on the water at Mobile Bay. "Come on in!" he bellowed. The west wind was howling as we set the tent up. We went to the end of the pier to watch another beautiful sunset. David and his wife, Mary, had us in for a vegetarian feast. I didn't think there were any vegetarians in Alabama. After dinner we ran out to the dock butt naked to watch the silhouette of the moon on the water. We had less than a month before we got married in Key West.

The next morning we put some sunblock on, stripped down to shorts, and pointed the machines east. Highway 98 was pretty quiet, which was good because they had forgotten to put a shoulder on it. Any car that passed us either veered into oncoming traffic or we bit the ant-infested ditch.

We crossed the state line into Florida. This no-shoulder thing was a new experience. Ever since leaving Vancouver we had always had some kind of shoulder. Here there was absolutely nothing. Three inches to the left and you were in traffic. Three inches to the right and you were in loose sand or dirt. Straying either way was extremely dangerous. For five hours straight we saw absolutely nothing except the white line on the highway.

Mentally delirious we arrived in Pensacola and crossed the two-mile Pensacola bridge. The winds shifted to crosswinds. Blowing off the Gulf those winds must have been doing at least forty miles an hour. The gusts kept forcing us into traffic. We had to lean into the wind to compensate. Then we got migraine headaches from the strong breezes blowing through our ears.

Once across the bridge the verbal assaults from the rush hour committee began. Four times side mirrors nearly clipped me in the head. It really seemed as if the drivers were out to get us. Our newest challenge: the hostile environment of Florida. Ten more miles of this basket-case highway and we were done. There was a dirt road that led us off 98.

We knocked at the door of a friendly looking house. Ed answered. Finally we'd found calm within the storm. Soft-spoken and friendly, Ed showed us where to set up the tent, then offered us a beverage.

At 5:30 A.M. Ed came out to offer us hot showers and some breakfast. Inside the bathroom there were two towels laid out, and two glasses of fresh orange juice

beside them. Ed and his wife, Lulu, made pancakes with fresh-picked blueberries. With all those nasty people on the highway, we still managed to find Ed and Lulu.

Back onto 98. There was a huge tailwind with ninety miles to go to see Deanna's mother, father, and brother in Panama City. About forty miles west of Panama City the traffic got really busy. We had two wide loads run us completely off the road. Then a barrage of cars yelling insults and coming within half an inch of us to wail on the horn and watch us jump. We hitched a ride off the death highway with a young kid named Scott from Alabama. He dropped us off in Panama City.

More cycling down 98 to get to Dee's brother Michael. Michael, 31, was really happy to see his sister. Crystal, Michael's girlfriend, was there with their new baby daughter, Autumn. They lived in a beautiful three-bedroom house, with a huge swimming pool. Deanna's mom, Cleo, came home from work and her dad showed up too. Mike and Cleo had divorced a few years back but still remained good friends.

While Dee was taking a shower the whole family shared their opinion on what Deanna and I had seen as her "awakening." They were very confused about why anybody would quit her job, give all her stuff away, and hit the highway. I could see where Deanna got her interrogation habits; the whole family barraged me with questions.

Eventually it became apparent that everyone thought there was something wrong with Deanna. I could relate to Deanna's family being so concerned. This beautiful

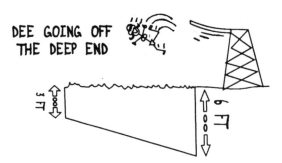

DEE GOING OFF
THE DEEP END

People as Friendly as Pitbulls with Rabies

woman who had been so stable just a few short months ago was now a traveling gypsy. We decided to tell them about our wedding plans at a later date.

Of all the challenges I had experienced on this trip, a non-supportive environment was the most challenging. We had planned to relax in Panama City but all this family stuff seemed more like a test.

We checked out the town and the beach. There were young people recovering from hangovers everywhere! The beach was magnificent: soft white sand, crystal clear water, and cloudy overcast sky. We rode back to the ranch for more food and naps.

At 7:00 A.M. the next morning we were at Power 108 radio station for an interview with Kelly and Rudy on the morning show. While Kelly was introducing me I went really wacky and started biting his leg. I like to do those things once in a while, just to keep things lively. I think I must have surprised him because he said, "Jesus Christ," live on the air. I don't think that's allowed in Florida.

Kelly and I really hit it off. Some radio jocks tried to crush me before I could get a word in edgewise. Kelly did a little teasing then let me tease right back. That moment in the studio stood still in time. I realized that being on the radio was a childhood fantasy. I had done so many interviews and had not even clued in to this.

That afternoon we went to Michael's shop to fax off press releases. While sending them out, Michael called Deanna over for a private talk. I knew something was up. Michael was having a really difficult time with his sister's outlook on life. Some more questions. "Are you doing something bad? You're so happy you must be doing something

DID SOMEONE SAY FANTASY?

bad. Are you worshipping crystals? Are you worshipping the devil?"

When we got back to the house the interrogation continued. Deanna's family has an incredible love for her and they seemed to feel left out and confused because of her new lifestyle. Crystal, Michael, and Cleo all had good intentions and were just dealing with their feelings.

Kelly had us back the next morning on the radio as guests. I continued to think about my childhood memories of the radio. When I was very small I thought that all the bands played live on the air. I couldn't figure out how they could set up their equipment so fast. Then I found out they just played records. All my life I have wanted to be a radio jock but had never thought I could do it.

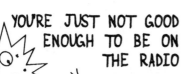

We rode back to the house and did our best job of being positive, but it didn't change things a whole lot. I felt uncomfortable about the trip, my message, being in Florida with Deanna's family, and having other people support me. I wondered whether I should quit the ride. Guilt and doubt were kung fuing it out in my head. I finally realized that my self-doubt was only because of all the concerns raised by Deanna's family. It seemed to magnify my own doubts about EnviroRide. The "mind poo" was getting louder and louder.

It seemed impossible to get out of bed in the morning. Where were all the happy people? If only there were some way to shift Deanna's family. We rode our bikes to Kelly's. He had been the only sanity in this town and he was crazy. He had arranged an interview with ABC news for us. Kristina, the reporter, raced out to meet us and we spent two hours taking shots, interviewing, and kidding around.

The next day we rode to the Panama City *News Herald* for pictures and an interview. Lori, the reporter, was fascinated with EnviroRide.

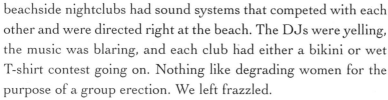

After we were finished at the newspaper we went to the beach. The two beachside nightclubs had sound systems that competed with each other and were directed right at the beach. The DJs were yelling, the music was blaring, and each club had either a bikini or wet T-shirt contest going on. Nothing like degrading women for the purpose of a group erection. We left frazzled.

We received some $250 in donations from our forwarded mail. We mailed $200 to Deanna's bank account and with the $50 left we headed towards the Keys. My body felt trashed. This week of rest had been more physically, spiritually, and mentally challenging than any part of the trip so far.

We arrived at Port St. Joe's and knocked at the door of Curtis and Diane. Diane had read the article in the paper and recognized us. They invited us in for dinner. After dinner Diane gave us slippers with little pompoms on them. It was a comfort to go from interrogation to free slippers.

Back out on the highway we had another new challenge. Deanna was experiencing chronic back pain. She had had back problems five years ago and I guess they had come back for a visit. She wanted to see a chiropractor but we couldn't afford a chiropractor. By four that

THE ANGRY NERVE DOG BITING DEANNA'S VERTEBRAE

afternoon Deanna could no longer ride. We found a state campground to stop for the night. After paying for the campsite and groceries we had only eight dollars left.

April 15, 1993. It was another beautiful day in paradise with our friends the gnats. They ate us while we ate breakfast. More flats. I just didn't have energy for riding. None. Zero. Deanna's back was killing her and I thought of ending the trip right there.

By 4:30 we were bagged. With only four dollars left we begged the forest rangers to let us camp for free. "Yes," said the dude with the really cool hat. Inside the campground there were three touring cyclists from Germany: Tobi, Ekhard, and Gerlinda. They had started in Germany, had ridden to North Africa, caught a plane to South America, then crossed the Andes and flown to Miami. They planned to ride to the Grand Canyon and San Francisco, fly to Japan, then finish in China. Made our little trip seem like a cakewalk.

The gnats were at an all-time high. Big thick swarms surrounded us. There were so many that they were flying in my mouth while I ate dinner. My ears were getting bigger and bigger from all the bites.

At the first light of day the ranger told us that there was a huge storm coming our way. The Germans went west and we went east. After ten miles the winds and torrential rain set in. There was no shoulder, no shelter, and no relief for at least thirty miles. We propped the bicycles up against a road sign and wrapped ourselves in the tarp hoping for a positive change. We soon realized we were standing in a fire ant hill.

People as Friendly as Pitbulls with Rabies

A little red pickup truck stopped to help us. Art and his family were going south and invited us to ride in the back. The bikes barely fit in so I had to sit on the tailgate. Art liked to drive about ninety miles an hour down the highway. With the rain whipping the back of my head, I held on for dear life praying Art wouldn't hit any large bumps. Above me, I could see the sky twisting and turning, waiting to give birth to a tornado. I was unsure which was safer, standing on the road, or riding with Art.

Art got us through the storm and dropped us off at a supermarket in Perry just off Highway 98. With our four dollars we purchased whatever we could in groceries.

We cycled south in between the pine trees that lined Highway 27 and the rain set in again getting everything wet, including our sleeping bags. We had to stop for shelter under the tower at a ranger station. BOOM!!! Lightning struck the tower. Sparks went flying, there was a sonic boom, and Deanna went white. We continued on and found Homer and Berdy's house.

They invited us in for a coffee and allowed us to dry our sleeping bags. Berdy opened up her heart to us and told us of her travels in years gone by. "I used to sleep in motels but you never know when a nigger's been sleeping in there!" Berdy said.

Now here's an attitude you just don't get to see every day. Friendly folk doing what they think is the right thing to do, hate people. Well, it sure was nice meeting you, Homer and Berdy, but we'll be outside in the pouring rain if you need us.

The Adventures of Coconut Head

The whole area felt very tense. I had thought that Louisiana or Alabama might be prejudiced but this was ridiculous. Almost every white person we met only had two questions for us: "Where you from? You got a nigger problem there?"

No, but Deanna's back was giving her some real problems. We found a chiropractor in Crystal River, hoping he could help her. He made us sit for an hour and a half in the waiting room. We told him the purpose of our mission and that we didn't have any money. He said that he completely understood and that he would take care of it. For only forty-six dollars he would adjust her and send us on our way. We left the office, tears running down Deanna's cheeks.

We traveled another ten miles with Deanna in horrible pain. We looked for a place to stay. A mobile home community to the left seemed like a good place to start.

The first house we checked had Harleys out front. Hmmm. Bikers. They should understand our situation. The yard was full of pitbulls and the trailer was full of bikers, seven of them. Black leather jackets, long hair and beards, big tummies, and big boots. Inside there were joints, beers, a standup bar, and four restaurant booths. "What is this place?" I inquired politely. "It's the clubhouse for the Iron Coffins Bike Gang!" said Popeye, the president of the club.

Carol-Ann, one of the "Ole Ladies," took Deanna aside. She let her use the shower, and shampoo, gave her a cold beer and some tender attention. At one point, Grump, the meanest, hairiest, smelliest biker, confronted me only an inch from my face and yelled, "Are you a cop?" Popeye jumped in

YOU DON'T HAVE $46? I GUESS DEANNA IS GOING TO BE BUSY CRYING ALL DAY WON'T SHE?

THE "DOC"

THE GUY THAT THOUGHT I WAS A COP

between me and Grump and yelled at Grump to back off his guests.

I was wondering how we had attracted this kind of support. I thought about the bikers, then Homer and Berdy, and all the other racists we had met over the last couple of days. These so-called "bad bikers" were the most normal people in this redneck wonderland.

As I dropped off to sleep fear came to visit. Will they get drunk and pull something stupid? What was I, crazy? We were personal guests of the president of the Iron Coffins Bike Gang. Nobody was gonna mess with us.

In the morning all the little Iron Coffins were still napping with their blankees so we tiptoed out of there. After a lunch of dry bread and peanut butter sandwiches we found a bank machine. The mailed money had finally made it to Dee's account. We could eat without begging. There was a local soccer team seeking donations at the supermarket. Without a thought I put two dollars in the bin. Lisa and I always used to share our cash with others. Dee and I had been sharing everything but our cash; maybe that's why we had run out.

The scenery went from pine trees to fast food outlets when we rode into Tampa. There were black people intermingling with whites, shopping in stores, applying for home equity loans. We had made it back to reality. Tampa was clean with palm trees in every direction. The key was under the mat at Matt's, a friend of Stephen, with a note that told us the name of their cat and the neighbors' dog.

Matt came home in the middle of the night and was gone to med school by 6:30 in the morning. Matt's friend Bill took us to the

THEY
CALL
ME
THE
"BANANA
MAN"

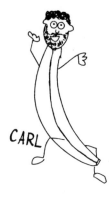

CARL

beach to kick back in the warm Florida sun. I always feel at home on the beach, as if I am some sort of reincarnated surfer.

Monday, April 19. We packed up and headed out of Tampa. Kent, a friend of Deanna's from Austin, had left a message that he wanted to meet us in Miami, which was still almost 300 miles away.

It was cooking hot out the next morning when we headed south on Highway 41 to see Dee's friend Eddie in Sarasota. Due to road construction the first ten miles of the road were oiled dirt. The fumes made my head go big and our tires kicked up a layer of grime that stuck to our bodies and our bags. Hot and tired, we stopped at a Circle K for a slushy. A friendly man in a green van stopped by and the next thing you know we were best buddies. He was the promotions man for Del Monte International and was sympathetic to our cause. The sun had been taking its toll on us all day so Carl gave us T-shirts and visors galore. He also extended an invite to stay at his house in Naples, south of Sarasota.

It was eight o'clock that night by the time we found Eddie's house. Eddie was an activist of sorts and also worked for the State of Florida as an environmental cop. He fines all the people that refuse to live in harmony with the Earth. Eddie also had an excellent sense of humor. One day he took a whole box of "Bio-Hazard" stickers and went to the local supermarket and pasted them on every loaf of white bread in the store.

I WILL
SAVE
THE
EARTH
FROM
WHITE
BREAD

EDDIE

We had a day's rest in Sarasota. I got on the phone to Key West to see if I could arrange a freebie motel for our honeymoon. Mike, the manager of the Eden House Motel, was also getting married that same weekend and said he would be happy to donate a room.

People as Friendly as Pitbulls with Rabies

We left Eddie's with eighty miles to go to Naples. As soon as we got back onto Highway 41 there were headwinds to greet us. For the last few days I had been in a trance, unable to enjoy anything. My head was filled with dark thoughts about all of Florida.

The busy highway, the aggressive drivers, and the elements restricted us to only thirty-eight miles that day. Just outside of Bayshore at a gas station we met Arlene, who offered us the use of a shower. Did we smell that bad? Arlene and her family also had us over for dinner, TV, and let us stay in the yard.

"This is the first time I've ever done this," Arlene said. "I don't even know why I asked you." I thought to myself, well, it's like this, Arlene. You, and everyone else on this planet are loving, generous, wonderful human beings. When you listen to your heart, nice things happen.

HEY MAN
WAKE-UP

The little birdies of morning woke us up. Arlene and her family were already dressed and ready to take us out for breakfast. We had breakfast, thanked them for their hospitality, and with our spirits boosted we returned to the narrow-shouldered highway.

A strong north wind pushed us a little closer to Karl's house. Until the sidewall of my rear tire blew out. The only way to fix it was with duct tape. Port Charlotte had a bicycle shop and David the owner donated a new tire. Even in all the weirdness of Florida, the basic human need of supporting other people was still shining strong.

The tailwinds blew us right into Fort Myers. We had a little break before starting the last eight miles only to find out it was actually forty miles. Pedal, pedal, pedal. Then the headwinds arrived to make us crazy.

We finally made it to Carl's, our Del Monte friend. Carl and his dog, Harry the Great Dane, greeted us at the door. Harry was a 130-pound monster, white with black spots and a head the size of

HARRY

REX

a tyrannosaurus's. On his hind legs, he stood at least six inches taller than I did. Carl was going through his third divorce. He participates in them so much, he must really enjoy them.

Carl cooked us an incredible dinner and then we watched *The Simpsons* from the master bed, all four of us (including Harry). Then we turned Carl's house into a biker circus with water guns and fancy kung fu moves. Harry was supposed to lie down dead after getting hit with Nerf darts but kept on knocking us off the furniture. I wondered if Carl's corporate days were numbered.

Friday, April 23. The next morning as we were leaving, Carl had a gift for us, a "Mrs. Coconut Head." Coconut Head now had a date. Wow!

It was hot, damn hot that day. You could have baked a cake in my sleeping bag and it was damn windy too. There was still no shoulder on the road and we were caught in morning rush hour. Car after car was swearing, honking, or scraping us. Then the Coke delivery truck ran us off the road.

Heat, headwinds, and I felt like I was getting a cold. We paused at a rest stop for a siesta but received twenty mosquito bites in five minutes so we continued. While riding Highway 41 we saw a lot of alligators. They just sat on the side of the ditch, soaking up the sun ten feet away from us. Interesting little creatures. Did you know they can run up to thirty miles per hour?

People as Friendly as Pitbulls with Rabies

By five o'clock we had cycled only thirty miles. We stopped at the highway patrol office for water. Captain Jeff Cox directed us to a primitive campground near Ochopee. The visor Carl had given me kept the sun off my face. That was good. The visor had not kept the sun off my now burnt bubbling head. That was bad.

EXTREME CLOSE-UP
OF MY EYE

We positioned ourselves in the campground right beside a twenty-foot trailer that was completely covered in murals of eagles, trees, and wildlife. Kim, sign painter extraordinaire, his wife, Lynn, and their two kids Leroy and Kim Jr. traveled all over the States with Kim picking up sign painting jobs as they went. He did this so he could spend as much time as possible with his children before they had to go to school. I threw some respect at him.

That night I also threw some respect at Mother Earth. She produced a sunset with bright hues of orange and red that silhouetted a long line of palm trees, with the moon suspended over top of them.

Before we left, Kim posed for a naked picture beside the trailer and wished us well as the headwinds got stronger and the air got hotter. After thirteen grueling miles of 90°F and 100 percent humidity, we couldn't take it any more. We found another primitive campground and put up the tent right beside a lake. As soon as it was up we crawled inside for a nap out of the hot sun. The wind howled and howled while inside the two overheated bikers were researching some rest. Upon awakening we discovered we had some neighbors, Matthew and Anne. Matthew told us of his time in the Marine Special Forces. He got to travel on special missions to kill people.

Anne finally changed the conversation. Guns were her favorite topic. I thought you two made a great couple. They demanded we have dinner with them. You know when you're so hungry you would eat anything? This wasn't one of those times. The salmon surprise tasted like snails and puppy dog tails. I wondered if this was how Matthew killed people on his special missions.

MATTHEW
AND ANNE

Just before bed, Richard, another camper we had met, offered us a ride into Miami. "You kids are going to have to ride through some pretty tough neighborhoods." I thanked him but declined. I wanted to ride my bike into Miami.

The next morning Richard persisted about taking us into town so we decided to take him up on the offer. We thanked Matthew and Anne and gave them a Hackeysack to remember us by. Then we loaded up into Richard's truck. He had to move his loaded handgun off the front seat so that I didn't put an extra hole in my bum. So many people owned guns out here. In Canada, I don't know one single person who owns a handgun. What do they do, give guns away as graduation presents? Is there any relationship between the out-of-control violent crime in the U.S. and the number of hand-guns? Richard dropped us off in a Miami suburb called Coconut Grove, at the house of Lani, a high school buddy of Deanna. The Universe had delivered an armed guard to ensure our safe arrival in Miami.

In the morning I phoned the media but no one was interested in our story. Now if we had been riding our bicycles around the country shooting people that would have been a news story. My imagination was running wild in Miami. Everybody must have a gun here. No people made eye contact; it was a stone-cold environment surrounded by palm trees and beautiful beaches. I wanted to go to Margaritaville to find Jimmy Buffet so he could marry us.

People as Friendly as Pitbulls with Rabies

Just before we left Lani's, Deanna's friend Kent hopped on his bike and joined us for our trip to the end of Key West, 156 miles from Gunsville. We took Highway 1 heading south to get off the mainland of the U.S.A. The farther south we got out of Miami the more intense the hurricane damage was. Hurricane Andrew had taken place nine months before and it still looked like it happened just yesterday. Malls, car dealerships, condos, trees, all had sustained major havoc. People's homes and communities were completely destroyed.

A NO CAMPING ZONE

Homeless people were trying to take shelter in the park. Except there was no shelter. All that was left were stumps; every single treetop was gone.

We cycled to Florida City, hurricane central, with very little money. We were looking at total devastation on both sides of the road. Every person that saw us glared angrily at us. We passed by a house with a prominently displayed sign that read, "No trespassers. YOU WILL BE SHOT!" Well, I guess we won't be camping there now will we.

Poor Kent. The first night of his bike ride and all it had been so far was danger and destruction. We set up our tents in a field that contained a flipped-over station wagon (a hurricane victim), a broken-down three-ton truck, and three-inch yellow grasshoppers on every blade of grass that surrounded us. We cooked dinner realizing that we were camped on a huge ten-foot-square anthill. We could deal with that, until the sun started to disappear. Then the cockroaches emerged, spurting this way and that way in the twilight. I had had just about enough fun for one day. Tomorrow we would begin riding into the Keys.

We left Florida City the next morning with a great tailwind. The three of us cruised at high speed for twenty-two miles and got off the mainland and on to the Keys. The Keys were beautiful with palm trees and crystal clear water, but the people were as friendly as pitbulls with rabies. It was like getting a wisdom tooth pulled.

The temperature was 87°F outside; we had to stop at a Winn Dixie for fruit and a chance to hang out in the air conditioning. Back on the road we started to overheat again so we jumped into the ocean for a delicious swim. There were no sandy beaches in the Keys, just coral dumping grounds. They are beautiful, but they were hell on our feet.

Right beside the beach was The Holiday Isle Resort so we sneaked into the pool and blissed out. We had a nap and a picnic lunch, and hit the road. Kent's knee was in agony, Deanna's back was making her cry, we were surrounded by angry people, and I was contemplating calling it quits in Key West. Get married, borrow money for a plane ticket and just shoot this crippled horse and put it out of its misery. But for today it was time to find some real estate.

SO GLAD YOU COULD MAKE IT

"Hi, can we stay in your yard?" I asked. "How did you get through the gate? Scram, beat it!" the twitching man said. We asked another. Same response. We asked seven different people and they all said, "NO!" Since I'd left Vancouver only three people had said that we couldn't camp in their yard. Now in Florida seven in one night. When the hurricane went through in 1992 many people migrated into the Keys. This influx of people had freaked all the locals out. There just weren't enough resources to accommodate everybody.

Then we found the First Baptist Church of Islamorada. Danny, the minister, and his wife, Marybeth, were glad to have us as guests. Showers, food, and good conversation. We finally found who we were looking for.

We posed for a picture with Danny and his family (with our clothes on), and then we all held hands and said a little prayer to the big guy. We thanked them and proceeded on with only eighty miles to go. It sure was nice to have Kent along with us. Houston was the last time we had had happy company.

The tailwinds were roasting and the scenery was extremely ravishing. Popsicle-blue water, green trees, and blue skies. The old highway had barely been wide enough for two cars, so many people avoided driving to the Keys because of the danger. Now the Keys had a new highway with big shoulders, making for safe bike riding.

FIRST BAPTIST CHURCH
OF ISLAMORADA

WE LOVE EVERYONE
INCLUDING BIKERS

BOOK OF HOSPITALITY 12:17

That night we ran into the same problem trying to find someone to let us stay in their yard. At mile marker twenty-three, however, we found a little path into the bushes that led to a camping spot by the water. Sheltered from the traffic, we were safe for one more night.

As I lay in the tent listening to the popsicle water slap onto the rocky shore, I thought about the experiences I had had on this trip. I had traveled 4,980 miles, and tomorrow I would be in Key West, Florida, the southernmost tip of the continental United States. I really couldn't give a damn. The trip was beginning to feel like punching a timeclock; it was hard to wake up every morning. Where had all the fun gone?

A CLOSE-UP OF THE OTHER BIKER AFTER WE SAID "HI" TO HIM

Another day of howling tailwinds. We sailed the last twenty miles into Key West. At the edge of town we saw another cyclist. When we said "Hi!" he told us "Go f#** yourselves." I guess that's how they say hi to each other in these here parts.

The Adventures of Coconut Head

We checked into the styling Eden House Motel. There was a beautiful outdoor pool sheltered by thick luscious palm trees. The room was a bloody apartment—an upstairs, a downstairs, a big balcony all compliments of the owner, Mike Eden, at the Eden House Motel (blatant advertisement). We cooked veggie burgers on the balcony then watched Homer on the tube. Aah, very styling.

We awoke very early for a radio interview with Chris Wolfe at WEOW, the Southernmost Rock Station in America. Another guest on Chris's show, Jack, invited us for a sunset cruise the next evening. I updated Z-100 in Portland, and four Vancouver stations: Andrea at Z-95, Larry and Willy at CFOX, Jacqui Underwood at Coast, and Geoff Palmer at KISS-FM. Continuing to encourage people while being totally discouraged seemed rather silly. I collapsed on the bed in a state of confusion.

FOR A GOOD TIME

CALL THE

EDEN HOUSE

Later that night we all went for a walk on Duvall Street. It was supposed to be famous for artists and creativity everywhere. The only creativity I could see was related to "Just how much money do you think we can milk out of a tourist?" Cheesy T-shirt shops, postcards, spoons, rides, photos, electronic shops, tacky, tacky, tacky.

The new highway and the recent installation of a cruise ship dock has brought in massive amounts of foreigners to this tiny little haven. Key West was a fantastic place, it just seemed a little imbalanced. Kent treated us for dinner at Jimmy Buffet's Margaritaville. We asked for Jimmy, but he was nowhere to be found. That night I sweated buckets. Here I was in Key West, about to be married, and I had another fever.

I spent most of the next day in bed until it was sunset cruise time. There was an overnight Fed-Ex package for us at the front desk. Carl had shipped out two blow-up Del Monte bananas for a wedding present.

We met Jack and went out on the catamaran. Being on the boat on the cool soothing water was such a relief. We had escaped the prison of bad thoughts on land.

Let's blow up the bananas and have some real fun. The last three months had started with the difficult riding across Texas and the headwinds of Louisiana, then the storm in Mobile, the challenge of Deanna's family, the unbelievable racism and hatred of northwest Florida, then the massive hurricane destruction and hostility of southern Florida. In between puffs of air I was trying to ask Deanna if she still wanted to get married when the captain of the boat started yelling at us.

"What the hell do you bring bananas on my boat for?" He was seriously pissed off that we had brought blow-up bananas on to his boat. It's an old boating superstition, something about the banana boats coming from South America that were contaminated with tarantulas. How were we supposed to know? Our little bit of fun was crushed by our paranoid captain. We had to put the plastic bananas away.

Deanna and I decided that we must get the hell out of this place and get married somewhere else. I couldn't really see ourselves having a happy wedding with people riding by on bicycles telling us to go f*** ourselves. We sat in total silence after the encounter with Captain Neurotic, waiting to get back on land.

The wedding was off, we were broke, Mastercard was on to us, and I wanted to end all this "bike adventure" crap right there.

Coconut Head: Rest in Pieces

Key West, Florida, to Salvo, Virginia

May 1, 1993. We thanked all the staff at the Eden House and headed out into the street. Kent had found a ride back to Miami because his knee was too painful to ride with. I was ready to quit but Deanna reminded me of the importance of EnviroRide and all the benefits it had to offer. When I had first started on the trip, all I could think of was how could I make this last forever. Now all I could think of was how could I make it end? I was almost in tears. It seemed like every rotten thing that had happened to us had been presented in virtual reality in the last week. I was watching two staff members joke around pushing carts into a grocery store. That's what I wanted. A job, a place to live. Hold it! Did I say I wanted a job? God, I was more depressed than I thought.

I phoned my mom for support. She had helped me through a lot of situations; certainly she could help here. Mom was sleeping, but Dad was there. He told me about the two friends of his that had died in the past couple of days. He also mentioned that he and mom were the only two "originals" living on our block; the rest had lain down to die. I tried to sound sympathetic but it was difficult because I was the one looking for sympathy.

We stopped at the Key West newspaper. Eric the reporter asked, "Why are you doing this?" I thought that this trip was as much fun as cleaning up fresh dog poo on a hot humid day. The more questions he asked, the more nauseated I felt.

I was at the farthest possible point away from Vancouver, and I was homesick, how convenient. We had gone only seven miles when Deanna's gear cable broke. This put her bike into the most-difficult-to-pedal category. Don't worry about that headwind, honey. It would be safe to say that the trip was not smooth and flowing at this point. Our intention was to make it back to mile marker twenty-three to our hidden camp spot. Deanna's broken cable was not helping. I put my bike in the same gear just to make it even and we trudged on.

We completed the last five miles on Highway 1 in the dark and the mosquitoes were out in full force. I had had more bug bites in the last month than I had had in my twenty-seven years of existence on the planet.

The message of EnviroRide was to ride a bike to help cut down on pollution. But surely we didn't have to die trying. Cars running us off the road, storms, and all the angry people everywhere—it sucked. We decided to get a ride the next morning and get the hell out of there. Hallelujah, angels sang, the bells rang 'cause we were getting out of anger jail. We were so physically drained we couldn't even make dinner.

I AM DOING THIS BECAUSE I AM HAVING SUCH A GREAT TIME

We left our secret spot without eating breakfast and phoned Kent, who was willing to come back to get us. I think I had psyched myself out about having to cycle through the rest of the Keys and then into the hurricane-ravaged areas. Kent arrived three hours later, we loaded up the gear, and headed back to Miami. Three hours of driving probably would have taken four or five days into the headwind. We went back to Lani's house in Coconut Grove and had the whole pad to ourselves because Lani had gone to New York. It gave us a chance to figure out whether to continue or go home.

THE RUN AROUND

There was a fax machine in the apartment so I tried the media again. Miami must have had a lot of crazies; trying to contact a radio personality in that town was impossible. Every time I called they gave me the runaround. After hours on the phone I finally gave up. I spent the rest of the day reading while Deanna and Kent went to the beach.

Unwilling to give up, I spent the next morning calling more radio stations, but they still treated me like a lunatic. I think the Universe was telling me to get the hell out of south Florida.

After a good night's sleep Deanna and I decided that we would continue EnviroRide as long as we left south Florida. The message was important. We were almost two-thirds of the way to Ottawa and Deanna had been such a huge pillar of support. What more did I really need?

May 5, 1993. The next morning Kent and I loaded everything into and onto the car so we could get out of south Florida as quickly as possible. We stopped at a supermarket in the retirement community of Hallandale. At the bakery a retired man and a retired lady started scuffling over who was next in line to buy some doughnuts. The store was bumper-to-bumper carts in every single aisle. I stopped too long to bargain shop and the lady behind me rammed me in the ankles with her cart. Another beautiful aspect of this state, speed shopping.

That evening we stayed with Deanna's school friend Lisa in Orlando. We woke up late the next day and headed over to the swimming pool at Lisa's condo complex. Lisa and Deanna had gone ahead and I got locked outside the

CAN YOU IMAGINE?

iron fence. It was a simple matter to hop over the fence and into the pool. Within a few moments, however, I was surrounded by stressed-out middle-aged people and an officer of the law. "Sir, you are under arrest for trespassing," the macho cop said. Somebody had been spying on me and told the police I was stealing a swim.

The lady with the biggest wrinkles on her face gave me a lecture for five minutes, even though I had every right to be there. This little incident was a pretty good reflection of the state. Why was everybody so gosh-darned pissed off? That night Lisa took Deanna out for a drink while Kent and I stayed at home and shared insights.

Talking with Kent I realized all the challenges I had built up in my head had no basis in reality. Sure they were real enough, but their impact didn't have to be real and they didn't have to ruin our trip. I resolved that from then on everything was going to be an easy deal.

Early next morning Kent drove us east to the coast so we could continue the journey from there. We stopped at the Loco-Motion Bike Shop to replace Dee's gear cable. Tom tuned up her bike and put the cable on for four bucks. My main sprockets, chain, and

YOU
ARE
UNDER
ARREST
TED

rear sprockets were completely worn out. Tom said I should have replaced them 18,000 miles ago. I was looking at over $200 to get my bike roadworthy. I also needed a new front tire; my tube was bulging out of the sidewall. With only thirty dollars, buying food was more important.

Kent dropped us off at the beach and we hugged good-bye and departed into rain and headwinds. It was now May 6 and we still had approximately 1,550 miles to make it to Ottawa and finish the trip.

After only twelve miles we were running out of daylight. We found a friendly looking house and knocked on the door. Robert opened the door and said it would be fine for us to camp in the yard. Both Dee and I were stunned, a friendly person and we could stay in the yard. Could it be true?

We ate, packed, and were on the road by eight the next day. Forty-three miles later we were in Daytona Beach. The beach stretched as far as the eye could see. We rode for ten miles right on the hard-packed sand, weaving in and out of the bikinis and ocean birdies.

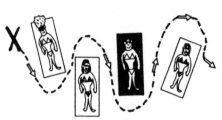

OUR BIKE ROUTE ON THE BEACH

We found a secluded spot on the beach to set up camp and rest our weary bodies. The sound of the ocean, the moonlit night, and the dancing stars. No Holiday Inn could ever match this. Except for one thing, the sand. The sand got into everything. Our shoes, underwear, and even our pancakes.

Pancakes, pancakes, pancakes. Was I channeling Aunt Jemima or what? With a large amount of flour product in my tummy we continued north on Highway 1. About 10:30 I was being sprayed with water from a passing car. It was Kent; he knew we would be traveling this way and just drove around until he found us. Kent was in between college classes driving around to see the country.

We continued on and found a picnic area in St. Augustine. Peanut butter sandwiches with fresh bread. Then a siesta in the shade. When I woke up I found that the birds had eaten all the middle parts of our bread. St. Augustine was a beautiful city. Architecture with class and lawns of green grass. The farther we got away from south Florida, the lighter and more friendly it was.

Eight miles out of town, Dee attracted a spike to her tire. I insisted she change the tire by herself. I could have helped her but you can give a man a fish or you can teach a man to fish. Whatever that means, she became "Bike Repair Woman."

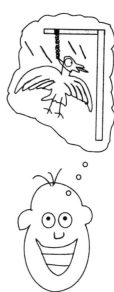

ME THINKING

We set the tent up so that as soon as we awoke we were looking at the sun peeking up over the horizon. Bright yellow, orange, and red showered our tent in the wee hours of the morning. We had a room with a view. After we packed everything up we stripped off all our clothes and went onto the A1A highway for a group naked picture riding our bikes down the highway. We hugged Kent good-bye again and departed.

The A1A Highway was lined with short palm bushes on each side of the road. Deanna's back was lined with pain on each side of her spine. The heat was hot. Made us dizzy. Felt weak. Kept sentences short. Need water.

We stopped at Nassau County Fire Station Number 2 on Amelia Island only five miles from the Georgia border. Bryon the lieutenant's diagnosis was that we had heatstroke. He offered us water and insisted that we have a shower. Well, twist our rubber arms.

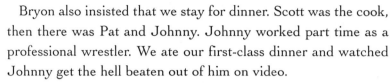

WOULD
YOU
LIKE TO
STAY
HERE?

OK

STAY!

JOHNNY

BRYON

ME
IN
THE
FIRE
TRUCK

Bryon also insisted that we stay for dinner. Scott was the cook, then there was Pat and Johnny. Johnny worked part time as a professional wrestler. We ate our first-class dinner and watched Johnny get the hell beaten out of him on video.

Scott loved practical jokes. He told me about one of his favorite gags on Rick, another firefighter. Rick would spend hours taking his target shooting gun apart and cleaning it. Then one week, Scott took an extra screw and threw it in with the disassembled handgun. Rick spent many days trying to figure out where the extra screw had come from.

Then Scott told us about another firefighter, Bill, who loved to keep his pickup truck in perfect working order. Scott would siphon five gallons of gas out of Bill's truck every three or four days. Bill couldn't figure out why his truck was getting such poor gas mileage. He rebuilt his carburetor, replaced the fuel lines, the filters, anything that would make a difference. A couple of months later, Scott returned all the stolen gas five gallons at a time, back into the gas tank every three or four days. Rick and Bill share a room in a mental asylum.

Before I left I asked Bryon if I could go up on the ladder truck. One hundred and ten feet up in the air was quite the experience. I could see miles and miles of country but I was more interested in hanging on as the adrenaline pumped through my bloodstream.

We waved good-bye to all the interesting, generous firemen and got back on the road. Highway 17 took us out of Yulee and across the Georgia state line. That was the day we finally got out of Florida. It seemed as if we had been there forever and now a concrete block had been lifted off my shoulders.

Coconut Head: Rest in Pieces

Deanna was not so lucky, her back still aggravating her to the point of tears. I was inspired by her continuing efforts to persevere. I had tried many hours of massage, love, sex, pancakes, nothing seemed to work. Even with tears rolling down her cheeks, she had never voiced a single complaint. She was slowing the pace down, but her spiritual strength more than made up for it.

SURE IT'S PAINFUL BUT I WILL NOT COMPLAIN

DEE

After two hours riding in the hot sun we found a spot for a break in Woodbine. Virginia, a sweet bubbly old lady, greeted us outside her store. We visited with her for almost half an hour. She did some of the most incredible paintings I had ever seen. All of us shared stories and our love for life. Even in the most difficult situations we still found a gleam of inspiration. Virginia gave us that motivation to keep going on in the 90°F heat.

We ate our last dry bread sandwich wondering where the hell we were going to get our next meal from. I checked the voice mail. My dad had phoned to say that he had put fifty dollars in our account because he had got his income tax refund back. It couldn't have happened at a better time. We hit the bank machine and headed for the grocery store.

GRAMMA SCHREDD'S DRY SANDWICH SURPRISE
INGREDIENTS:
1 LOAF OF UNSLICED BREAD
DIRECTIONS:
SLICE INGREDIENTS AND SERVE
IF BREAD IS ALREADY SLICED
JUST SERVE

The store had a little table in the back and AIR CONDITIONING! A lady approached us, "Where are you going with all that stuff on your bikes?" Anne gave us ten dollars and a knife carved from stone. Then we met James on the highway who invited us to set up in the backyard. He gave us a two-liter bottle of Pepsi and a cooler full of ice. It was free cash and soda day!

I like to get up when the sun rises, Dee likes to sleep a little longer. When I tie her to the bike and ride around the yard a couple of times she usually wakes right up.

DEANNA'S MORNING WAKE-UP CALL

We went to the laundromat in Brunswick. Nobody was around so I put on my last clean underwear and T-shirt and loaded all our stuff into the washer. As soon as the washer started people came in droves. They were all looking at me, pointing and laughing at the biker boy in his underwear.

DEE

BEFORE REN

AFTER REN

Right beside the laundromat was the Dr. Ren Halverson chiropractic office. Deanna wanted to check with the doctor to see if he would help. There was a nice feeling walking into his office. We asked for the doctor and he took Deanna by the hand and immediately put her on the adjusting table. It was going to cost $47.50 for an adjustment but with the money from my dad and for the sake of Deanna's sanity we had to do it.

My knowledge of chiropractors was limited; I had never actually seen one in action. Well, Ren got in there and started wrenching Deanna's body around. Every move he made Deanna would squawk in amazement and relief. Every time she screamed I would break out laughing. Ren did about fifteen different little adjustments. Adjust, scream, and laugh. If there were any new patients waiting in the lobby, I am sure they ran away.

Afterwards Dee had the look of total relief in her eyes. What a relief for both of us. It had been hard to cheer Deanna up while she was suffering so much. We approached the counter to pay the bill. "Don't worry about it, this one is on me," Ren said. We hugged the good doctor good-bye. We purchased groceries, film, and sunblock. Our cash balance was fifteen dollars.

Fifteen miles later we had cycled to Darrien, Georgia. Dee went for a walk while I cooked up some spaghetti for lunch. Ten minutes later she came back to say that one of those so-called rednecks had been following her in a Camaro.

"He was trying to impress me by saying, 'hey baby,' and 'Wanna go for a ride?' Then he spit hot dog chunks and spilled his beer on his shirt!" I chased after him, flexing my thighs, grunting and screaming. He quickly took off.

The neighborhood had a definite racist feel to it. The white areas didn't like blacks and the black areas definitely didn't take a shine to us. We found a church to camp at. Tom, the minister, showed us where to tent and was unseen for the rest of the night.

We needed some toilet paper so we went to the corner store. When we walked in, nearly every person in the store was staring at us. It took me a few seconds to realize that we were in the black store. Whities went across the street and black folks shopped here. The United States, land of opportunity, land of truth and liberty for all. Which category does racism fit under? I fell asleep in a state of shock that human beings like to segregate themselves due to physical appearance. I believe that people everywhere are just human spirits with different kinds of body bags.

We left the church heading on our way to Savannah, Georgia. Dee's back was considerably better but there was still some soreness. Every five miles we stopped so she could stretch her back out. By 11:30 she was totally in tears again. I comforted her with hugs as she cried and spit out delusional theories on how she was wrecking the trip. I suggested a hotel room at this point and Dee was happy to oblige.

THE STORES
WE VISITED

GROCERY
WHITE FOLKS ONLY

GROCERY
BLACK FOLKS ONLY

Deanna woke up the next morning with grizzly beavers of pain chewing away at her nerve ends. We charged another night at the hotel room without the credit card checker thing.

YOU GUYS STOP HURTING DEANNA

ME LECTURING THE GRIZZLY BEAVERS

The next morning Deanna was feeling better so we rode to downtown Savannah only three miles away. We checked into a bike shop and met T.C. Pipkin, an environmentalist. It had been so long since I had seen an environmentalist I had to be reminded what one was.

T.C. was a university graduate and ex-oil field worker who had thrown it all away because he saw firsthand some of the vicious corporate damage in the name of making money. I think it is impossible to rape the Earth and have a peaceful spirit. We visited and encouraged each other for almost an hour before we hit the highway.

Ever since Austin, the land had been like a flat line on an electrocardiogram, but man they had wild bridges! One was almost two miles long with no shoulder and semi trucks galore. We barely survived the trip across into South Carolina. The temperature was cooking out and so were we. There were gambling casinos and fireworks outlets everywhere.

EVEN WHEN I FLIP MY SANDWICH, IT STILL TASTES THE SAME

We camped in a wooded area that night and rode north towards Charleston, South Carolina, the next morning. The first part of the day was on Highway 17, which paralleled I-95. The smell of the pines, the songs of the birdies, and the open road.

As 17 veered east, so did the traffic. It was time to

focus on that little three-inch white line and keep riding there for the rest of the day. Some people came up right behind us, wailed on the air horn, then zinged by at seventy-five miles an hour. Even though there was no traffic in the other lane the trucks still came within an inch or two of us. After miles and miles of trees, swamp, and buttheads, we realized we were very low on water.

At the junction of 303 and 17 there were a couple of houses. At one of the homes there was a retired woman sitting in a sundress on the porch. "Excuse me," I said." Could we have some water?" "Sure," she replied. We started filling up our water bottles with the hose when some dude out of nowhere started ragging us out. "People around these parts don't just help them-

selves to water!" His hand was resting on a handgun underneath his belt. "Well, actually the lady said we could help ourselves!" I said. "Oh . . . Would you folks like to come sit inside and have some apple juice?" the gunman asked. Now that was a shift in attitude.

WHO
WANTS
SOME
JUICE?

Our conversation over dinner with Rej the gunman took us in many different directions, from painting pictures to pregnancies resulting from incest in this state. After thanking our armed host, we retired to the tent for the night.

The gnats had a population of about fifteen billion in Rej's backyard. By 7:15 A.M. I had gone crazy from the bugs. We skipped breakfast to get away from them. Then we had twelve miles of verbal biker abuse from the passing vehicles. The temperature was rising one degree every five minutes and the humidity felt like it was a hundred percent. Horseflies were landing on my back, my arms, or flying into the side of my face doing some kind of crazy punk-rock horsefly slam dance. Deanna's back was in constant agony, we had no money, and the chain kept falling off my bike.

SID VICIOUS IS DELICIOUS

A PUNK ROCK HORSEFLY

We went to the newspaper in Charleston. They looked at us as if we were selling vacuum cleaners. I guess a 6,000-mile bike ride is a common occurrence. Well, that seemed to be a standard east coast response so far. "Save the planet? Hell, we're trying to save our navy and army bases so we can destroy the planet!" "What about future generations?" "We're trying to milk the earth for everything we can get." "But what about your kids?" "They can milk it too!"

I didn't want any of this mentality brushing off on me. I was having enough trouble worrying about the King Kong bridge over the Cooper River. After negotiating raging crosswinds, trucks, and shoulder debris, though, I figured I could do anything.

I DRIVE
EVERYWHERE
AND I MEAN
EVERYWHERE

After surviving the bridge we found a Bi-Lo grocery store. With our last fifteen dollars we purchased the most for the least. Outside I watched as a lady with five kids walked out of the grocery store and went to her car. After strapping them in, they all drove a whole twenty feet towards the hardware store. Then she got out, unloaded the kids and went into the hardware store.

Towards the end of the day just off Highway 17 we found the Awendaw Fire Station #2 nestled in the Francis Marion National Forest. Cody the captain invited us to sleep inside because there was a storm coming. Staying at a fire station was the most friendly, most comfortable environment we had found on the trip. It felt as warm as your own home. I think the firefighters appreciated it too. They had someone new to talk to besides themselves.

May 20. The next morning I made French toast for everybody. Cody made up a care package of tea, coffee, and gum. Deanna dressed up in a full fire suit, then choked me with a fire hose as the other firefighters stood and watched. Just for a picture, though.

As soon as we got back on the highway Dee's back started giving her pain. It had begun in Austin and had never really gone away. Despite the warmth I was feeling from the friendly firefighters, I started freaking out about everything again. I wanted to quit. I didn't want to see Deanna suffer any more. We made a left turn, traveled for a couple of miles, then found a state park.

We napped for a good hour in a screened picnic area. The ranger told us where the camping was and the cost was FREE—another three miles west to Elmwood Campground. It was used only during hunting season and was completely empty. There was a table, a big pile of firewood, and a water faucet right at our site. There was even a shower connected to a tree.

After sitting for a couple of minutes in the quiet I realized why I had been going crazy. I had been surrounded by people, traffic, and chaos for too long. I needed that nature buzz, the quieting of the trees, birds, and crickets. Each moment that went by I became more and more relaxed.

We had to turn the stove on and off while we cooked pasta to conserve as much fuel as possible. Outside it was pitch black except for thousands of fireflies surrounding us while we ate. We made a batch of popcorn and took the lawn chairs towards the trees.

The show was absolutely amazing. Fireflies filled the whole area, from way down the meadow to right in front of our eyes. Our tent had a big screen door and screened sides and we

TAKE OVER FOR ME WILL YOU?

GHOST OF C.H.

OK

MRS. C.H.

had set it up so we could see the fireflies from where we lay in bed. It was a 180-degree natural cinema.

Rested, and in a better state of mind, we headed for Georgetown. Riding felt good that day—the earlier connection with nature had really helped. While riding Highway 17 Coconut Head fell off the bike into traffic and, SPLAT, a semi truck ran him over and smashed him into a hundred pieces. He was at least twenty years old. That's 140 in dog years and who knows how many in coconut years. Mrs. Coconut Head told us that she would be willing to take on the role of mascot.

A couple of miles later at Litchfield Beach we stopped for a coffee at the local store. A drunken man approached us and would not let us leave until we all sang "On the Road Again" holding hands. Then he proceeded to take a pee inside the ice freezer. Fortunately we were not buying any ice.

Carl left a message on the voice mail to say that Del Monte was cutting us a cheque for $500. We were ecstatic. We had lost Mr. Coconut Head, but we had cash on the way. In Surfside, Mike the fire guy let us stay behind the fire hall.

The next day we rode into Myrtle Beach, a grossly overdeveloped tourist town. Every block had either a mini golf course or a warehouse-sized tacky T-shirt shop or both. Up ahead police

I CAN'T WAIT TO GET ON THE ROAD AGAIN

ICE ICE

were blocking the road. The Shriners were having a parade to raise money for sick children. They were dressed up as hillbillies, morticians, frontiersmen, pirates, cowboys, and clowns, each with a matching vehicle. They let us drive the World's Longest Bicycle (twenty-six riders) for the start of the parade.

We spent our last two dollars on food and we now had eleven cents. We made it into North Carolina and took Highway 139 to Calabash. This was the thirteenth straight day of riding since leaving Orlando.

We stopped in Ocean Isle Beach for a sandwich. Two problems: the bread had dried out in the sun and it had got squished in my bike bag. It was a pitiful sight peeling off micro-thin slices of bread from a glop of dough. Our sandwiches looked like they had been run over by a bus.

Riding through the residential area we found Harry, who invited us to camp in an open lot next door to his house. His wife, Ruby, came by with a care package. Spaghetti, garlic toast, and apples for tomorrow.

Just before we got into the tent, Harry offered their double bed in the extra room. Ruby came up to say goodnight. "Harry offered us the extra room," Dee said. Here was a stunning quote: "Yer not gonna kill me are ya?" Ruby pleaded.

We went into the house and Ruby whipped up more food for us. "I ain't prejudiced, but I don't like black men touching me," Ruby said as she handed us our plates. "Well, it's just the way I was brought up." Just because you are brought up a certain way, does that mean you have to be that way forever?

In Canada I had always felt we had just Canadians. In America everybody had a label. There were Afro-Americans, Latin

Americans, Native Americans, Jewish Americans, Anglo-Saxons and every other group out there. Why was everybody focused on how different they were from each other?

In the middle of the night, I heard a knock. It was Ruby. "I can't sleep. You can sleep out on the porch or I can help you set up your tent. I'm sorry, I feel so stupid, I just can't sleep." We were getting kicked out of the house in the middle of the night because Ruby thought we were going to attack her. We ran out of the house laughing.

BEAT IT YOU HOSE HEADS

HA, HA, HA, HA!

At the first light of day we made the fastest departure EnviroRide had ever seen. Visiting with someone who thinks you are a murderer just didn't seem comfortable.

We rode till noon and caught a ferry from Southport over to Carolina Beach, North Carolina. Fourteen straight days of riding and we had finally made it to Agnes's house. I had first met Agnes at the Quantum Leap seminar. A sweet woman who greeted us with kisses and big hugs. Thoroughly exhausted, we were unable to do much visiting. We wished everyone good night and re-treated to the tent.

The next day Agnes found a package in her mailbox for us. It was from Carl and contained six T-shirts, one pineapple carving knife, two visors, two hats, one cooking apron, one tea towel, one Del Monte watch, and assorted key chains. Carl was genuinely crazy!

The next day I took an early morning walk on the beach by myself while Deanna slept in. It felt good to hang out with the waves while Deanna caught up on her Z's and rested her back. Agnes offered to take Deanna into the chiropractor in

Wilmington. Agnes said she would pay for it and we could reimburse her later. She also paid to have the laundry done, stocked us up on groceries and fed us like kings. Agnes was a saint. Let's call her Saint Agnes.

Aaah, some more time to myself. Deanna's ongoing back torture was bringing up some questions. Could she finish? Would we need to slow down so she could heal? Should I go ahead and let her catch up by bus? Should she go back to Austin, go back to work and send me her paychecks? After a good long walk on the beach, I firmly decided that I wanted her to be with me no matter how healthy or gimpy she was. This suffering woman was the foundation of inspiration that kept the trip going.

Before we departed, Saint Agnes gave us a bag of oranges, a bag of kiwis, and a check for fifty bucks. The bells in heaven were ringing. We rode all day in thick traffic. It was like crossing the Grand Canyon on a tightrope; don't slip up or you're dead. We found the Ogden fire station where we could sit down and pick up the marbles we had just lost. The firefighters were happy to let us stay in the back. We ate dinner in the front seat of an old, abandoned firetruck as the sun gravitated towards the earth.

The firefighters had a call at about 4:30 A.M. That was some kind of alarm clock. I thought the firetrucks were going to drive right through the tent. The next morning we took Highway 70 towards Ocracoke Island. The road took us through a marine base that had signs like, "Tank Crossing" and "Live Artillery Flying Over Road Day And Night."

We had made it about fifty-five miles and stopped for some water. I looked out the window of the convenience store to see another touring cyclist. Al, fifty-eight years old, was riding from Fort Myers, Florida, to Maine, then home to Minnesota. My first impression of Al was that he had lost some marbles in traffic but had forgotten to collect them back up again. Every question I asked him he would laugh then avoid giving an answer. All he could say was that he wanted free camping and that he was coming with us. Each time I said good-bye to him he would express his desire to hang with us. After numerous attempts to depart without him, he was riding with us.

We found a church to camp at just outside New Bern. James, one of the neighbors, was incredibly happy and friendly. He offered some Coleman fuel that he had found the day before in the garage. James was concerned that since he had bought it twenty years ago it would be past the "Best Before" date. "Pour some on the ground, and light it up," he insisted. So I lit the fuel and it worked. This made James very happy.

We all sat outside the tent talking and managed to squeeze out of Al that he sometimes rode a hundred miles in a day. Deanna and I, the young, athletic types, were having our butts kicked by this fifty-eight-year-old dude. You know why? He had had a lot more time to train!

Al was one of those guys you'd like to get a lab coat, a government grant, put him in a glass room, and study him for a year or six.

We were on the road by 7:00 A.M. the next morning. The tailwinds gave us a boost and we made forty-five miles by 1:00 P.M. The ferry to Ocracoke Island was at three o'clock. With thirty miles to go, we decided to go for it.

Coconut Head: Rest in Pieces

We raced towards the ferry while the road wound east, west, north, and south. We pushed harder and harder to make it there by three. As we pulled onto the deck, all the people that had passed us on the road in their cars were clapping. We had made seventy-four miles in eight hours. Yahoo!

Ocracoke was a sandy, relaxed island off the northern coast. People were walking, families were cycling on both sides of the road, and the state campground was full. Luckily, a group of cyclists who had paid for ten campsites was willing to share.

We were in the middle of "Friendlyville." In every direction was a picnic table surrounded by tents. Our great tent, which I was so proud of, was dwarfed by all the six-person bungalows around us.

Even though we had raced for many miles in the hot blazing sun I hadn't seen Al take a single drink of water. He wore blue jeans, long shirts, and wore his helmet for hours after he got off his bike. Then he would hang out over my shoulder without talking or even laughing at my cheap jokes. We had extra refried beans, so I made Al sit down and eat some. He hadn't eaten anything since breakfast. I was concerned about our fellow biker. He chowed dinner with us still wearing his bike helmet.

HA, HA!

TOOT
TOOT

AL AFTER DINNER

It was a fairly cool night but we had no desire to retreat to the tent. The conversation with our neighbors was too interesting. The whole time we were visiting, Al was standing by his tent just gazing into the distance with his helmet on. He went to bed as the sun went down, while we stayed up socializing.

The wind howled all night long. When I popped my head out of the tent at the first light of day, I realized it was blowing steadily from the north. Many tents had collapsed, including Al's. Dee and I decided not to risk further aggravating her back riding into this wind. Hopefully Al would continue along by himself. I loved Al

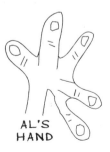

AL'S HAND

but I felt the difference in our personalities made it uncomfortable for all of us. I changed my tires around as Al got ready for departure. He finally left, giving us a good dose of relief.

After a day of rest the wind had died down and it was just ten miles to the ferry from Ocracoke to Cape Hatteras. The highway was deserted, with only the odd bunny chewing grass on the side of the ditch. The forty-minute ferry ride was quite spectacular. The seagulls hovered right behind the boat, waiting for an offering from the generous tourists. They hung in the air as if they were tied to a string on the back of the boat. Some people think these birds are a nuisance but I think they are poetry in motion.

YUM, YUM

A BUNNY EATING

Cycling north towards the Cape Hatteras lighthouse, a friendly young man came to ride alongside us. Eric, a graphic designer from New York, was fascinated with what we were doing. We instantly became friends, chitchatting along the way.

Eric wanted to tag along with us to check out the lighthouse. It was the first time this 200-foot-high building had been open to the public since 1986. It was now 3:00 P.M. and the lighthouse closed at 3:30. We raced full bore to get there. Completely out of breath, our legs cramping as we climbed to the top, we finally looked out onto the shimmering blueness of the Atlantic Ocean.

Right beside the lighthouse was a turtle pond and we could see fifty little turtle heads poking out of the water. We sat on the bank and all fifty of them surged towards us. Turtles probably don't get as many grains as they should so we fed them some whole wheat bread. They crawled over top of each other jockeying for that whole wheat flavor. The clunking of their shells and their snapping little mouths will stay embedded in my brain forever. We hugged Eric good-bye and continued on.

Twenty miles later we found the Salvo Volunteer Fire Department. Ritchie, the captain, was there with about ten other guys for training night. Realizing there was a big storm coming, Ritchie told us to set up our stuff on the floor and sleep inside.

We had the fire hall all to ourselves. Training night was over and all the firefighters had gone home. For at least twenty minutes, Deanna and I sat looking at each other in shock. Ritchie must have really trusted us to have let us run rampant in the fire hall. We cooked dinner, cleaned up, and had a quick naked picture on the side of one of the trucks. The storm raged outside and we drifted off to sleep.

As I lay on the hard concrete floor, a thousand thoughts of doubt were arm wrestling in my head. I still didn't know what to do with my life. What kind of work would I do once I got home? Where was home? Back in Vancouver, or somewhere in between here and there? Did Deanna want to be a part of my life? Did I still want to be a part of hers? Will Mastercard ever find us? There was only about a month left for EnviroRide. I told the Universe that I was ready for some answers any time now.

IT RAINED A LOT THAT NIGHT

On Our Last Leg

Salvo, Virginia, to Ottawa, Ontario

Tuesday, June 1, 1993. We had had a tailwind almost every day in May and had cycled 775 miles, but we were still more than 900 miles from Ottawa. Hopefully we could make it by the end of June. The Salvo Fire Hall had kept us dry all night but we had to face the elements once more. There was an ice-cold headwind from the north so we took shelter at the Down Under restaurant and we drank coffee until noon but there still was no change; we had no choice but to leave the restaurant and slug it out with nature.

A few hours later we finally made it off Ocracoke Island. We rode along SR 168, passing through the first farmland we had seen in months. The corn, potatoes, and tomato crops were just being planted and the smell of freshly mowed lawns permeated the air. But there was something strange in among the grass. It was gravestones. I counted at least a dozen homes where people had buried their dead right in the front yard.

We looked for a camping spot in a gravestone-free zone. The whole "up yours" attitude of the south had really shaken my belief in my "Can I camp in your yard?" abilities. At one time I could stop at any home, in any town, and ask for a place to camp. But now, it just didn't seem that easy.

We pulled up into the driveway of a modest home and a little girl yelled for her mom to come out. Nora, her daughter Tiffany, husband Gary, and son Gary Jr., all said it would be fine for us to stay.

Gary Jr. and Tiffany came out to visit while we set up the tent in the backyard. These kids, ten and thirteen respectively, were just so excited about their new friends. They told us about trips to Washington, D.C., Gary's kidney infection, and how to drop eggs off ladders.

WANT TO SEE MY INFECTION?

GARY

Gary and Nora gave us the utmost respect. They told their kids that this was a once-in-a-lifetime opportunity to meet people like us. I was very honored. Maybe we had inspired somebody.

Then the giving excitement began. First they gave us a pen, a T-shirt, a vest, and then a sweater. Then Nora gave us three more sweaters, T-shirts, and stuffed animals. We retreated to the tent with twenty pounds of dead weight.

We left our generous hosts and eight miles later we were over the Virginia State Line. We picked strawberries for lunch. Eat three, one in the basket, eat three, one in the basket. It's a great way to get cheap fruit, and a sore back.

IF I GET PICKED I DIE

We arrived in the city of Virginia Beach and found the Old Davis Corner Rescue Station. Larry, the captain, invited us to tent around back. Tanya the firefighter gave us cool fire shirts. Mary, one of the medical volunteers, offered us a private room with a shower and fresh towels. Was this a five-star fire hall hotel or what?

The next morning Channel 3 TV came out for an interview, then we were off to the Chesapeake Bay Bridge, a bridge twenty miles long with two one-mile sections of tunnel. Built in 1964, it cost $100 million. As we arrived at the toll gate, five employees rushed towards us screaming, "Stop! Stop! Stop! You can't cross this bridge. No bikes are allowed!" So we stuck our thumbs out and made a sign. An hour later Dave took us across in his truck.

On the other side of the bridge, a huge shoulder appeared as wide as a whole lane. Deanna and I could finally ride in safety and talk to each other. After about fifteen miles we pulled up a long driveway surrounded by wheat fields on both sides. Knock, knock. I could see someone in the house but they wouldn't answer the door. I usually answer my door when someone knocks on it. Fear was alive and well in the rural areas of Virginia.

The next place we tried, Eunice answered the door. "Sure," she said, "Just camp over there," she said pointing to the right. Pointing to the left she said, "These folks inside won't mind, they're really quiet!" That's because they were dead. We were staying at a funeral home.

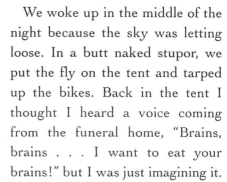

We woke up in the middle of the night because the sky was letting loose. In a butt naked stupor, we put the fly on the tent and tarped up the bikes. Back in the tent I thought I heard a voice coming from the funeral home, "Brains, brains . . . I want to eat your brains!" but I was just imagining it.

We survived the night and said good-bye to Eunice and all the quiet people and were on the way to Exmore Elementary School. Throughout the trip we had talked to schoolkids about our adventure. I think it is the children of the world that will be the pivotal factor in saving the Earth from being destroyed by mankind.

The principal was so thrilled about us speaking to the kids that he immediately assembled sixty students in the auditorium. I like to get people excited. The kids were raising their hands, shaking, and vibrating to see who could have their question answered. I encouraged them to shake and vibrate more, which angered some of the teachers.

WOLF STUFF

They wanted to know if I was a werewolf (because of my hairy body) and if Deanna was a cheerleader (because of her long legs, curvy figure, and rah-rah personality). At one point I got the kids so excited that when I asked for a group picture they thought "picture" meant "stampede!" One kid tripped the oldest teacher and gave her a fat lip. We wished everybody good-bye as blood dripped from the face of the country school teacher. I learned a valuable lesson in that school: teachers bleed too.

RAH! RAH!

We laughed all the way down the country roads. As we rode we passed huge, beautiful churches with stained-glass windows and cemeteries right beside them. Quaint little farmhouses and unique, small towns. Twice after rest stops, Deanna headed south when we departed. I was glad I was the navigational advisor.

We found Paul and Shelby's house, a retired couple who let us camp by their fishpond. It was full of bullfrogs cranking out their little froggie opera. These were no ordinary frogs, they were Steroid Baritone Frogs that kept me awake all night long.

The Adventures of Coconut Head

DANGER

WIENER
REJECTS

FOR
SCRAPPLE
USE ONLY

When we came in the house the next morning Paul was cooking up some scrapple and bacon for breakfast. It was my first encounter with scrapple, a grayish combination of pork parts that looked like it was made from wiener leftovers. I had to decline.

Out on the adventurous highway again we crossed into Maryland. My compliments to the Maryland Department of Highways—we rode on a new paved shoulder wider than a car lane. A warm tailwind made the ride that much more enjoyable.

The shoulder was great but it couldn't do anything for my bike. It was badly in need of some attention. The sprockets were completely worn out, the chain, the tires all needed replacing. I was waiting for the Del Monte money to fix it, but it hadn't made it to our account yet. The chain was so worn out that it would fall off many times a day. When it did fall off I would shift the gears, pedal really fast and the chain would be convinced back onto my worn-out sprockets. Only advanced life support could help my bike now.

Salisbury, Maryland, had a bypass or we could go through town. At first I thought the bypass would enable us to make some miles, yet my intuition told me to go into town. Our shoulder disappeared, putting us right into the thick of the traffic. Again, my intuition kicked in and encouraged me to get off the highway. We found a road that paralleled the busy street, keeping us in a northerly direction.

I HAVE
A GREAT
IDEA.
GO INTO
TOWN!

INTUITION

Mark and Maury, two mountain bikers, stopped to chat about the bloated appearance of our bicycles. Mark immediately offered us his backyard to camp in. Great!

When we arrived, Mark noticed my worn-out gears. He took a closer look and said. "Leave it be. I work tomorrow and will be able to fix this thing much easier." Mark was a bike mechanic at Salisbury Schwinn. My intuition had been right on target.

Six hours of labour later, this is what Mark had done: new free wheel, chain, chain rings, brake pads, gear cable, pulleys for derailer, repacked bearings in the pedal brackets on front and rear wheels, six new tubes, repaired my computer mount, three patch kits, new rear axle, a major tune-up, new tires for both of us, and free coffee. Over $300 worth of repairs. I was quite shocked, and so was Deanna. He gave my bike a triple bypass all for no charge. I phoned the local newspaper to share with them how generous Mark had been, then cooked him a meal fit for a king to thank him for his kindness.

The next morning we took Route 9 towards the Cape May ferry. The ferry cost eight dollars each, which was fourteen dollars more than we had. Our only option was to ask fourteen people for a dollar each. Deanna got completely embarrassed because we had to ask for money from complete strangers. But in fact 50 percent of the people we asked gladly gave the dollar. Within about thirty minutes we were on the ferry to New Jersey.

Dusk had begun to close in on us when we stumbled on to Billy and Fred. They were planting sweet potatoes on a plot of land just behind their house. We had dinner and crashed in the field.

The next morning Deanna explained to me her weird obsession with wanting to drive large machinery. Deanna asked Fred if she could drive the tractor while Fred and Billy planted sweet potatoes. They said, "Sure, why not!" Deanna had a smile so big her whole head was stretching trying to accommodate it.

That day was Atlantic City, the Boardwalk, the birthplace of Monopoly. We made it to town and turned right to get onto the famous boardwalk. Walking our bikes, we were surrounded by people questioning us: a complete press conference with questions flying at us like Patriots at a Scud.

Deanna had never gambled before so, with our last quarter, she went into Trump Plaza to play the slot machines. She returned a few moments later with a quarter in hand. She had plugged twenty-five cents in the slot, lost it, and found another on the floor.

We scooted out of there while we were on a roll to continue the journey into Atlantic City rush hour traffic with road construction to boot. The center lane was closed so we christened it Official Bike Lane. After ten miles of that, we stopped at a gas station for water and a rest. Highway 9 north was like the Florida roads. No shoulder and aggressive drivers. We gave up for the day.

Rita allowed us to camp in the yard. Her son, Tom, came by about an hour later. He was visiting with his mom because only last Wednesday her house had been robbed. An amazing exercise in trust for her only six days later to let two strangers hang out on her property.

YOU TAKE CARE OF YOUR PARTNER OR GO DIRECTLY TO JAIL

The sun was shining as we departed lovely Rita's. I was about a quarter mile ahead of Deanna on the highway when I looked back to see a cop pulling me over. He stopped to give me hell because he thought I had abandoned my riding partner. After my near arrest we spent the rest of the day trying to find a bathroom. New Jersey is a state where most gas stations only have restrooms for employees, no exceptions. What a strange challenge that was.

I NEED TO PEE
BY TED SCHREDD

THY PLACE TO PEE,
IS NOT FOR ME,
ONLY FOR THY EMPLOYEE,
EVEN WHEN I BEGS,
I HAVE TO CROSS MY LEGS,
THEY DON'T EVEN CARE,
IF I PEE OR WHERE,
I RIDE INTO THE DISTANCE,
A MESSAGE OF PERSISTENCE,
I NEED TO PEE,
O WOE IS ME,
I NEED TO PEE

We had a newspaper reporter interrogate us in Tom's River and we continued north on Highway 9. Somewhere along the path we stopped to phone our New York contacts, Bill and Roseanne. We were instantly surrounded by ten to fifteen Jewish people, young boys and old men. They all had matching outfits that I had never seen before. The boys had the Aunt Jemima pancake-shaped beanies and the men had black suits with magician hats.

They asked us questions for over forty-five minutes. One gentleman asked us the same question more than a dozen times. "Why did you leave?" No matter how we tried to explain he just couldn't grasp the concept. As we left the gas station I looked over my shoulder and that one man was still yelling at us, "But why did you leave?"

BUT WHY DID YOU LEAVE?

North of Freehold we found a place to camp on the grounds of a large seminary. Father Williams said if the storm got too radical we could sleep inside. Calling anybody Father is a trip. I don't even call my dad Father, I call him Dad.

Father Williams invited us inside so we could make our supper. We cooked dinner in the kitchen just as a meeting ended. By the amount of beer cans and wine cooler bottles, it looked more like a pub than a church meeting.

One man said, "God damn!" after finding out how far we had traveled. I thought saying "God damn" was like a big "Not!" in the church. I guess the commandments only applied when he wanted them to.

THE MAN WHO SAID "GOD DAMN". HIS IDENTITY IS ANONYMOUS SO GOD CAN'T GET HIM

Thou shalt not kill (unless it's a holy war). Thou shalt not take the Lord's name in vain (unless something you hear really surprises you). And, thou shalt not commit adultery (unless she has really great boobs). Whatever the rule, there always seemed to be an exception.

We left the House of God and edged towards New York City on a wide, freshly paved shoulder. The commuters had only two northbound lanes to fight it out on the way to work. Sometimes this wasn't enough. To change lanes they just pushed into the car beside them and that car would abruptly veer onto the shoulder. As we got closer to the city, the hills picked up and so did the danger. Both of us were completely freaked out by the enormous amount of traffic.

Bill and Roseanne had offered to pick us up once we had had enough. Roseanne appeared with her Subaru station wagon in the suburb of Elizabeth and we loaded the bikes in a frenzy. The highways had little toll booths every mile it seemed. Is this highway robbery? Ten tolls later we were home in Rutherford, New Jersey.

Bill, an MD, came home with their eight year-old-son, Max, and daughter, Allison. We all watched *The Simpsons* and called it a night.

The next day at Max's school there was a parent-student-teacher meeting. Roseanne had phoned Max's teacher to see if we could come out to speak to the parents and the kids. We only had about ten minutes to talk, so we went full out. Dee and I wanted to avoid any more teachers getting fat lips. It was quite different having the kids and parents together. I stressed the importance of making the world a better place to live. The elderly teacher in charge told us we had done "A-plus excellent" on our talk.

TIME OUT.. I NEED A BANDAID

The bikers and the family went to the video arcade after a hard day of school. There was one game that had two guys fighting each other with chain saws. Cut his arm off, blood gushes everywhere, but he could still fight with the other arm. Whatever happened to Pacman?

The next morning was filled with the sounds of breakfast and the loading of the van for a mountain adventure. We were off to see some friends of the family, Peter and Allan. They lived about an hour's drive out of Rutherford in the mountains separate from the psycho-spasmic tollways of New Jersey. When we arrived the birds were chirping, and the gorgeous trees welcomed us.

The air reeked of life. We spent the whole day lounging, resting, and relaxing. Allan had a bag full of deluxe sparklers that shot orange and red colors. I put "Neutron Dance" by the Pointer

The Adventures of Coconut Head

Sisters on the portable stereo and turned it up really loud. All the kids, the bikers, the adults, and the neighbors ran around spinning, twirling, and sparkling to the music for half an hour. Afterwards, we all hugged good-bye and made it home by midnight. I felt fantastic. OK, OK, I was blissed out.

Sunday morning Roseanne came downstairs with five twenty-dollar bills. "Here, Bill and I want to give you this. We want you to go have some fun in the city." Wow, a hundred bucks. We took the bus to the Port Authority, a four-story structure with buses arriving and departing in every direction. Down, down, down to the subway. Many faces, styles of clothes, and attitudes in every direction. I felt cramped, crowded, and claustrophobic.

The movie industry had me convinced that the subway was a home for nasty gangs and murderers. I made Deanna hold my hand and lead me through the danger zone. We finally found the right platform and the smell of urine was overpowering. We jumped on the train, and as we rushed through the different stations, I expected a holdup or Charles Bronson to smash through the window and shoot the suspect.

We got off at the World Trade Center and took an elevator ride 107 stories up. We were so high up that what appeared, appeared so small it was as if we were looking at a fake city. The lack of clouds in the sky made it easy to see the Statue of Liberty and the whole New York area.

Back on the streets there were tourists everywhere. Arabs, Orientals, Europeans. Every flavor of human being was represented. There was also garbage everywhere.

We found the ferry that went to the tall dame but the statue wasn't that impressive. Every time I go to visit somewhere, this is the weird pressure I put on myself. See this, see that, you should do this, you should do that, you should do everything. All these things cost money, you get to jostle for position with a bunch of tired, cranky tourists for a millisecond of satisfaction, then pay more money to get away from the cranky tourists, which means more jostling. The most fun in life comes from people and nature. Trees, turtles, fireflies, happy faces. Besides that, they are free. I can enjoy them wherever I go.

THE STATUE OF LIBERTY

Dee and I walked through Chinatown. People were selling everything imaginable to anyone who would buy. Little tables covered with shoes, shirts, underwear or watches, jewelry and ginseng, even furniture. Yes, furniture. Chinatown felt wonderful. I couldn't communicate with anybody, yet I felt they all were my friends.

We walked back to the subway past the famed corner of 42nd Street. A huge neon sign, four stories high, lit up the street. The Sony display had a television two stories tall broadcasting CNN. Featured were some riot police beating the shit out of some demonstrators. It was like a big brother scene with violence being the message.

Street hustlers were getting people to pick a card. I saw $300 change hands in less than ninety seconds. The hustler ran off and got lost in the crowd at the scent of a cop. Violence, gambling, and drugs surrounded me as I longed for turtles, fireflies and curly ocean waves. Back on the subway, then to the Port Authority for our bus.

Bill dropped us off at the outskirts of the big city. We spent the night with the friend we had met in Cape Hatteras. Eric lived in Beacon, which wasn't frightening, but his neighbor who raised snakes for a living was frightening. Snakes don't have legs but we had one more leg of this trip, from Beacon to Ottawa.

The Adventures of Coconut Head

The next day was Deanna's birthday and we were on the road again. She had been hinting every day for a month. With our limited budget I was unable to buy anything for her. What I really wanted to get her were some balloons. Five minutes after that I saw real estate signs on the side of the road covered with helium balloons. Thank you, Universe. I took a few and tied them to the bikes and I sang "Happy Birthday" to her riding down the highway.

We rode into Poughkeepsie and I took Deanna to Denny's for her free birthday lunch. About five we arrived in Rhinebeck. This town's claim to fame is it has the oldest operating pub in North America. On the street we met Harvey. He invited us over for dinner and allowed us to camp in his yard.

Harvey was a buyer and seller of antiques, and he seemed like a great guy. But the more wine he drank, the more crazed he got. Harvey was weirder than Al, and he had a mean streak in him. He went on about all the misfortune in his life and then tried making the moves on Deanna. This was not what she had been expecting for her birthday. We got out of the house and zipped ourselves inside the tent as fast as we could.

The next morning we went to Harvey's house to use the bathroom. In the kitchen stacks of molding dishes piled with cigarette butts were sitting on the floor, on the counter, and in the sink. Broken glass lay everywhere. Where had he cooked our dinner last night? What had he served it on? Why were we here? We left as quickly as we could.

INSIDE HARVEY'S SINK

The highway ran parallel to the Hudson River. Beautiful rolling hills on either side of a twisty river. I had no idea upstate New York was so beautiful.

We found John, who let us camp on his property on the side of the highway. We got some water from him but the sulfur taste was so strong it was undrinkable. The bugs were still abundant. Bite after bite on my neck and arms. This trip had been a once-in-a-lifetime experience but the bugs had to go.

We left early in the morning on the way to Albany. While riding down 9J beside the mighty Hudson I heard somebody playing the saxophone on a deck in the early morning sun. I would never have heard something so beautiful if I had been driving in a car.

About fifteen miles from Albany Dee started to feel dizzy. We stopped at a store and she disappeared into the bathroom for half an hour. We finally made it into Albany after stopping at every bathroom along the way. By the time we made it to the center of town, Deanna was completely diseased.

She lay on the grass in Washington Park, moving only to make it to the toilet. Deanna slept and I tried to

DEE FEELING DIZZY

figure out what the next step would be. Eric, another cyclist, came up and inquired if anything was wrong. I told him what we were doing and that my riding partner wasn't feeling too well. "Here are the keys to my apartment and my address," Eric said. "I'm going to work now, but I'll return tonight. Help yourself to food or drink and get healthy." It never ceased to amaze me how incredibly generous people could be.

Eric lived about six blocks from the Capitol building up a steep hill and I was wondered if Deanna could make it. She nearly blacked out trying to ride so we walked together instead.

When we arrived at Eric's, Deanna collapsed onto the couch. I made her tea and sang songs to her until she felt better. Eric came home from work about ten, made a quick sandwich and left for his other job. He only slept four hours a night. Eric, could this be too much? People made this bike trip out to be a big deal. Working two jobs, going to school, having children, having to commute, or working at a job you hate, now that's hard work.

THE JOB
MONSTER
CHASING US

We woke up and Eric offered to let us stay longer, but Deanna was feeling much better. Eric made us breakfast and sent us on our way with a Walt Whitman poem book to remember him by.

We traveled north on Highway 4, arrived in Glenn Falls about four o'clock, and set up camp beside a large industrial complex. It rained on us during the night and was pouring when we got out of the tent in the morning. We searched for cover. A strip mall provided us with shelter for five hours. It's a tough life when you have to live at a mall. We phoned our parents and Dee's family was relieved that she was OK.

Cold, wet, and bored we got back on the highway. Just as we pulled out the rain stopped. The Adirondack Mountains were spectacular, the low clouds wrapped them up like birthday presents. Deanna was very excited about her maiden mountain voyage.

We barely made any miles that day. Around Pottersville we asked the Universe if we could please have a warm place to stay that night. Two miles down the road a little yellow pickup truck pulled us over. Gary offered us a warm place to sleep and a shower. What the hell is this? Magically we asked for him and there he was. They work, they work, those miracles.

He threw our bikes in the back of the truck and he took us home. His wife, Lorraine, showed us to the deluxe spare bedroom and made us choose what to eat for dinner. Then Gary did a minor tune-up on Dee's bike and bought a newsletter subscription. This was not the worst treatment we had had.

GARY

Lorraine and Gary made us breakfast and a lunch for the road. Wow! We used the $20 for groceries and continued on. All day long the bugs attacked us constantly. When we had reached hurricane strength insanity we asked Phil and Doris if we could camp in their yard. Phil, a total redneck, called Connie Chung "an out and out lesbian that Commie Chung," and invited us in for dinner and to sleep in the extra bedroom. At one point during dinner, Doris told us she loved to drink the warm portions of butter you get when you eat lobster. Yum-yum. Phil snored so loud that Doris left the TV and radio blaring to cover up the snoring. It was a strange night.

PHIL'S NOSE THAT SNORED

June 22, 1993. 6,400 miles traveled during EnviroRide, and only 350 miles to go. The next morning we headed towards

Canada and the sky let loose with claps of thunder and screams of lightning. We took refuge under a bridge until it cleared up.

We spent our last night in the good ol' U.S.A. camping on the lawn of Dave and Kathy's house. I was looking forward to getting out of the United States. I had been almost nine months in this country, and I was impressed by the generous people who had crossed our path but I had had enough guns, fear, and prejudice to do me for a long, long time.

We flipped our pancakes through the air into our mouths and wished the family well. The day before we had done a newspaper interview. We grabbed a paper and read the reporter's perception of our interview. "Ted and Deanna admit asking restaurants for scraps more than once," it read. Restaurants had donated meals but never scraps. In fun we rode through the streets of Chazy yelling "scraps," hoping that someone would flick scrambled eggs at us.

The headwinds blew up again and the seven miles to the border seemed to take forever. We pulled up to the Lake Champlain border crossing, wondering what was going to happen. We had no money and I was importing a nurse. We got all our documents ready and rode up to the booth. The lady with the average-sized head didn't ask any questions and ushered us through.

Yahoo! Back in my beautiful country. Like all the things I once took for granted, I had forgotten how laid-back and neutral Canadians are. The customs guard's personality was a perfect example. She was warm, friendly, and didn't carry a gun. The American customs agents carried big guns and a big attitude. It just felt safe, knowing that the crime and guns were all behind us.

The winds continued in our face. Deanna went on strike because of all the physical torture. We talked it out and just kept hammering into that wind like our immigrant forefathers once did. We rolled into my cousin Alex's downtown Montreal apartment about 8:00 P.M.

June 24, 1993. The next morning we got to check out the streets. Montreal is a hip groovin' town. This place had girls with purple hair, it had culture! It was Saint Jean Baptiste Day, a French celebration of their identity, and there were bands and street performers and Quebec flags everywhere. After dinner Alex took us for a bike ride through Old Montreal. The city was hundreds of years old. Even riding after midnight we felt totally safe, even in the darkest parts of town.

That night I couldn't sleep because we still had not figured out where to go after the trip. I started to question what I had done to Deanna. Just a few short months ago she had had a successful job, car, and all that other stuff you are supposed to have. Now she was thousands of miles away from home. I stopped thinking and let the Universe deliver the answer. I never knew what was going to happen till it happened. Why start now?

Next morning Alex went to work and we did an interview with CBC Montreal. I also updated Z-95 FM in Vancouver. Andrea Ring pulled an incredible interview out of me. She complimented me on my crazy communication skills and suggested I start a career in radio. That was it! Radio! Right then and there I decided I wanted to be on a morning show in a big radio market. Sure, I didn't have any training or real experience but those were details.

Alex took us out to dinner when he got home. My cousin's never-ending generosity continued. We cycled to the Olympic Place Stadium for a look and convinced Alex to pose for a naked picture. "Only if you don't tell Auntie!" he said.

The next day Alex continued to give us more cash and quarters to do laundry. Later that evening there was an international fireworks competition.

We took our lawn chairs and our stove to the show and cooked popcorn right in the middle of thousands of people while we watched a half hour of spectacular fireworks. When they were over, we bolted on the bikes out of there. The traffic was gridlocked for cars, but not for us: a classic example of how great a bicycle is. We were long gone while the masses duked it out for the pavement.

On the way to Alex's we did a little urban riding. That's where you ride as hard and as fast as you can through large traffic jams. You must be fully attentive as you jockey for position in among all the large smelly polluting hunks of metal. It was such a rush for me to go twice as fast as a car.

The next morning we left for Ottawa to see my sister and my Auntie and finish EnviroRide.

We followed the eighteen miles of bike paths that snaked the canals to get out of downtown Montreal. There was even a bicycle ferry that took us across the Ottawa River.

It was another hot sunny day with strong headwinds. The universe was going to test our little asses right to the end. Bumpy roads and humidity, and after fifty miles we were bushed. Michelle and Andrea let us camp in their mosquito-infested yard.

We left early into more headwinds. Riding along the highway we noticed something was following us. Blackbirds. For some reason they thought we were threatening them so they had started taking dives at us. Maybe they were gang birds with nothing better to do.

We took a ferry back over the Ottawa River to Quebec and rode on the other side for a while. A bridge took us back into Ontario. We had two days left and we still hadn't received our cheque from Del Monte. After many long-distance calls we discovered it had been deposited in the wrong account.

We found a quaint little farmhouse on the side of the road. Clint and his wife, Mary, said they didn't want us staying in their yard. We were just about to go back onto

STAY THE HELL AWAY FROM ME!

MAMA BLACKBIRD

the highway when Clint came running after us. "You can stay if it's only one night." What was he thinking? That we were going to build a log cabin and raise some pigs? We had a sunset dinner for the second last day of EnviroRide.

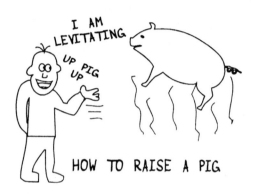

HOW TO RAISE A PIG

We split early so Clint wouldn't get paranoid. My head was reeling—all I could think of was radio and how I knew I had to work on a morning show. The elements were definitely challenging us every step of the way. There was another strong headwind after breakfast. I was looking forward to staying indoors for a month or two. In a house with screens and central air conditioning and heating. I wanted a stove that worked. When I peed in the middle of the night it would be in a toilet. I wanted to go for a car ride.

I WAS DREAMING OF THIS

We made it into Ottawa with relative ease. We got directions at a gas station and headed to our very last stop. The bike route led us through the spectacular Ottawa River valley. We passed by the governor general's house and the prime minister's pad. Pretty swanky places. One of them even had those guards with the red jackets and really big heads. Then the House of Commons. What a bureaucratic wonderland.

We arrived at my Auntie Marion and Uncle Connie's house excited and confused. What the hell were we to do now? We retired to the extra bedroom and considered our options about what to do with our lives.

We were up at six o'clock for an interview. At the studios of Rock 54 the announcer asked the question I still couldn't answer, "What are you going to do now?" Afterwards, we went to the post office and opened our forwarded mail. A Mastercard bill, a Visa bill, all kinds of bills, $100 in cash donations, and a package from California. Inside were five gold rings. Shelley and Klaus, some friends we had never gotten a chance to visit on the West Coast, had also included a note. "These rings are to be used to trade for meals."

That night we went to see the RCMP musical ride. Our national police force had a group of beautiful horses and incredibly talented riders. We sat in lawn chairs and ate a picnic dinner as the horses trotted around to music. "Do any of the RCMP drive cars?" Deanna asked. We packaged all the newsletters when we got home and called it a night.

July 1, 1993. Canada Day. We headed towards the heart of the city where hundreds of thousands of Canadians were wandering streets filled with food, singers, jugglers, and entertainment in every direction. On the way back downtown we saw hundreds of people riding their bicycles. We went back to the Quebec side of the river to watch the fireworks explode over top of the Parliament Buildings. It was a magnificent way to end an epic journey.

Next morning I made Deanna breakfast in bed. Still we didn't know where we were going to live. We had accomplished our goal yet we had so little. All this time of lack, at least we had had a destination. Now we didn't even have that.

We went to the post office to mail off the newsletters and checked the bank machine to see what was happening. We had a huge balance. The Del Monte cheque had made it! The $500 American had converted into $650 Canadian. What were we going to do? "Let's ride to Vancouver!" I bellowed. "Yee-ha," Deanna replied.

AFTER THE BANK MACHINE

Ted and Deanna's Highway Nuptials

Ottawa, Ontario, to Vancouver, B.C.

July 2, 1993. My bicycle odometer read 6,812 miles. The whole east coast had been effortless. It was still about 2,800 miles back to Vancouver but ever since we had left Florida we had been having a great time. We haven't been caught riding in the rain since April 10! I was feeling vivacious, with all the exercise, sunshine, and the solution to my career search. Now with all this money both of us were feeling on top of the world.

Deanna and I were very excited as we packed up to hit the highway again. There was a magnificent cloudburst with lightning and heavy rain that disintegrated just as we were ready to depart. My sister Helen and her husband Brian rode us out of town to Kanata and sent us on our way. Every single day in Canada there had been headwinds. That day was no exception. The headwinds picked up considerably as the afternoon wore on and our bikes were loaded with groceries. I stopped at a food bank bin just to make my bike a little lighter.

By 5:00 P.M. we stopped at a dairy farm exhausted. Katrina and Fred showed us where to set up the tent. Our hosts took off to a dinner party while Deanna and I made love in the hot summer sun. The cows mooed in approval. A big, healthy dinner while we reflected on the joy that my relatives and the last two Canadian cities had brought us.

At 7:00 A.M. we were on the road. We crawled at a snail's pace, accomplishing only eighteen miles by 10:30. I was ready to pass out and so was Deanna. We crashed for thirty minutes right there on the gravel shoulder of the highway as the semi trucks raced by. Back on the bikes, I wondered if there was a single person I knew that might even consider taking a nap on the side of a busy highway.

THOUGHT FOR THE DAY:

DON'T SLEEP ON THE ROAD

We slugged on. About two o'clock I heard a weird noise behind me. I looked over my shoulder and saw a car heading right for us, one of its front wheels completely gone. A bright orange ball of sparks was coming from the out-of-control vehicle, which was now within inches of us. The loose tire rolled into the opposite ditch at sixty miles an hour. What could a fully inflated tire bouncing at high speeds or a three-wheeled car do to us? I was highly impressed that the driver chose to stay on the road and not to treat us like bowling pins. I wondered what the Universe was trying to tell us.

DANGER! DANGER!

Ted and Deanna's Highway Nuptials

We kept on cruising. The winds finally stopped around four o'clock. Both our butts were tender and sore after seventy-five miles. We found Thomas's house in Chalk River. Thomas started with his personal medical history, the heart operations, the kidney stones, the drugs, nursing care, and so on. I quickly responded with all my ski injuries, every time I had had the flu, and every bandage I had ever worn. Not wanting to be outdone, Thomas went into all his neighbors who had died. I attacked back. I didn't have a lot of death stories but my dad sure did. I suggested they get on the phone and duke it out to see who knew the most dead people.

MOSTLY I LIKE TO TALK ABOUT PAIN, MISERY, AND DEATH

THOMAS

A new day, new adventures, and new bugs. Blackflies were the new villains. Twice the size of gnats, these little bastards went unnoticed until blood dripped from the wound and a small welt developed. Deanna ran frantically around the yard trying to pack as Thomas slipped in a dead neighbor he forgot to mention the night before.

Lots of big hills to start our day and the blackflies followed us. I didn't even need my speedometer any more. If I traveled less than twenty miles an hour, the black-flies were around. Less than eighteen miles an hour, the horseflies and deerflies were slamming into my face, my ears, my eyes, and up my nose.

A BLACK FLY

We made forty miles by noon. The temperature was increasing and we were completely out of water. We wanted to stop but I thought just one more hill. It was three miles straight up. I had a heat flash, felt dizzy, and almost fell off my bike. I waited for Deanna at the top. She said she was hallucinating, seeing water on the side of the road. Considering we were out of water, it was a good thing to see.

The Adventures of Coconut Head

WATER PLEASE

We were on the King's Highway, Highway 17, and there hadn't been anything but trees for the last thirty miles. We found a rest stop but it had no running water so we had to beg for some water from some travelers. We were delirious; a nap was in order. We lay down in the shade but the damn flies and mosquitoes attacked us. We had to set up the tent to escape.

When we woke up it was at least 95°F out. A strong headwind blew up, making it even more nauseating. We packed up the tent with blood dripping from our blackfly bites. Any normal human being would have gotten on a plane and flown home after sleeping on the highway.

At Deux Rivières we took shelter from the heat in a restaurant. Outside an hour later the wall of heat knocked us over. The creek beside the restaurant was brown and littered with floating debris, but it was either that or heatstroke. As we climbed out of the creek a woman watching us said she had quit swimming there because one day there were bloodsuckers in her hair.

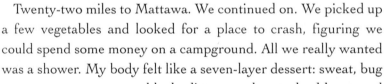

A BLOOD SUCKER

Twenty-two miles to Mattawa. We continued on. We picked up a few vegetables and looked for a place to crash, figuring we could spend some money on a campground. All we really wanted was a shower. My body felt like a seven-layer dessert: sweat, bug spray, sunblock, dirt, car exhaust, dead bugs, and creek slime.

The campground wanted fifteen dollars, but on the edge of town Mrs. Dubois let us camp on her bug-infested land for free. I overspiced the food and ruined dinner. Between my dirty body and the humidity I felt like glue. We had to sit naked in the tent to keep cool and stay away from the

DINNER TASTES LIKE POO

I CAN'T STOP SWEATING

THE BUGS WAITED FOR US TO PEE

bugs. Hundreds of mosquitoes sat outside ready to pounce on us as soon as they had an opportunity. We were having a great time.

I had gotten a good dose of heat stroke, physical exhaustion, and dehydration. My body then went ahead and petrified on me overnight. The day before I had drunk ten bottles of water but it wasn't enough. I was wandering around like a zombie when I got out of the tent. Mrs. Dubois invited us in for a shower. Thank God.

BEFORE MY SHOWER

By 10 A.M. we were on the road with a fresh twenty-mile-an-hour headwind as soon as we hit the highway. In the last couple of days it seemed that with each moment that went by, the challenges had been growing by leaps and bounds. I asked the Universe if this was necessary. After a whole half a mile we found a restaurant to sit and drink coffee in until our energy was restored. Well, the wind blew even harder with rain and lightning.

AFTER ONE SHOWER

Have I mentioned what a great time we were having? Three hours later we departed the restaurant. We decided to splurge on a campground. At a slow crawl, we made it to the Samuel de Champlain Provincial Park. I took three cold showers before I finally felt like a human being again.

AFTER TWO SHOWERS

The bugs were still out the next morning. We had to wear layers of clothing to protect ourselves. If I turned the wrong way, a blackfly would get into my shirt, up my back, or in my hair. It's hard to describe just how damn annoying this was.

AFTER THREE SHOWERS

July 6, 1993. More headwinds but they weren't strong enough to blow the damn flies away. Back on Highway 17 climbing the first pitch I asked myself a few questions: Was this bringing me maximum joy and aliveness? Was this the best use of my time right now? Was there any value living in the breeding grounds of

THIS SUCKS

the bugs from hell? Could I take 2500 miles more of this to get to Vancouver?

We should have just quit in Ottawa as we had planned. The tire falling off the car, the heatstroke, the headwinds, the exhaustion, and the f#**ing bugs all added up to the very clear message from the Universe to call it quits. Deanna agreed. We both had a firm belief that if it wasn't fun, why bother? EnviroRide was done.

It had been an inconceivable journey that had tested every aspect of my soul. Hurricane-like storms, gale-force headwinds, torrential rains, strange people, guns, guns and more guns, bad food, no food, no water, bugs, killer fish, and fearless raccoons. I had seen the lot. I had learned so much about myself and this wonderful world we live in but I was ready to throw in the towel. We had accomplished our mission. We really didn't know where we were going to live but I definitely wanted to be with Deanna. I suggested we go to Vancouver and see if she liked it there.

We pulled the bikes over and stuck out our thumbs. Only a small percentage of the traffic was capable of giving us a ride since we had all our stuff and our bicycles. Yet in less than two minutes a truck stopped to give us a lift. Lynne was on her way to a family reunion. "Well, I can give you a ride to Winnipeg, then I'm going to North Dakota." We were back in the flow again.

Two days later we arrived in Winnipeg. Lynne gave us $20 for a newsletter subscription and wished us luck. We stayed in town with my friend Gloria, then we cycled out of Winnipeg and started to hitchhike the next morning. Making signs, singing, and dancing just wouldn't get us a ride. We tried turning a bike upside down to get sympathy. That didn't work. We had to beg on our knees before somebody finally stopped. We traveled 370 miles to Regina and paid for a hotel room.

That next morning our destination was Edmonton to see my family so they could meet Deanna. We loaded up the bikes and cycled to the edge of town. Two hours later Gilbert, a university professor from Missouri who had recently shaved his head, was heading to Alaska so he took us right to my friend's front door in Edmonton. We had traveled from North Bay to Edmonton in only four days. That would have taken at least a month on the bikes.

On the drive into Edmonton we thought it would be kind of neat to get married in town. All we wanted was a simple wedding, nothing fancy just a "Do you? And how about you?" Then we would be legal and could have cheaper car insurance rates!

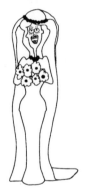

ONLY
$4000
BRIDE
NOT
INCLUDED

Call me crazy but I think a wedding is supposed to be a happy occasion. Almost every wedding I have ever been to included one or all of the following: a stuffy ceremony where most of the guests were bored to tears; financial and emotional stress for both families; wedding vows that say, "Honor and Obey, or Till Death Do Us Part." Those vows were written hundreds of years ago when controlling people was a good thing. After that everybody has to sit through a bunch of stuffy speeches before the dancing and fun begin. That's why they invented honeymoons, so the stressed-out wedding couple can avoid mental breakdown. Dee and I decided to get married the simplest way possible.

The next morning we went to my parents to break the news. My mom got so excited she was asking about rings and cakes and ceremonies and all kinds of wild tangents. All I really was concerned about was that there would be enough cupcakes for everyone.

MOM AND DAD AFTER THEY FOUND OUT ABOUT THE WEDDING

The Adventures of Coconut Head

On Saturday, July 17, 1993, we had our wedding. Deanna was icing the cupcakes as the justice of the peace was walking up the steps to my parents' house. We got married on the front lawn, which overlooks the winding North Saskatchewan River valley.

My two brothers from Vancouver drove out and my sister flew in from Ottawa. The whole family was there, even Betty my dog, who was a bridesmaid. We were married in our bike shorts by the JP. I wore my One Less Car T-shirt and Deanna wore a casual blouse. We tied beer cans to our bicycles and with "Just Married" signs we rode up and down the boulevard in front of my parents' house. The photographer was my oldest brother Jim (who I think is better than Ansel Adams).

BETTY ALWAYS CRIES AT WEDDINGS

With $500 in wedding money we saddled up the bikes one more time. Edmonton to Vancouver was about 750 miles. It would be our cycling honeymoon home.

Leaving Edmonton we had a lot of media coverage. The story now was the wedding, and radio, television, and newspapers all covered it. Rick, a college teacher, heard us on the radio and gave us a $100 wedding present. The written story was carried on the Broadcast News wire service across Canada. They called it a "Harlequin Romance." Our television interview was carried by satellite across the country. Had we known how much publicity a wedding would have caused we would have done it sooner.

We rode through the Canadian Rockies seeing bears, squirrels, mountain sheep, and all kinds of other wildlife. Incredible mountain vistas, spectacular weather, and financial abundance. This was the first time Deanna had ever seen the Rockies and this kind of wildlife. I had seen these mountains a hundred times before but seeing Deanna's wide-eyed look of awe made this trip feel as if it was my first visit as well. We met Rob, a freelance reporter for the BBC of London, out in the middle of nowhere. He interviewed us and sent our story overseas.

We arrived in Vancouver on August 13, 1993. We had massive radio and television coverage upon our arrival. CBC-TV, Z-95.3 FM, CFOX, QM-FM and many other media organizations covered the story!

After 8,178 miles, thousands of pancakes, experiences that defied imagination, and a new marriage, I was finally home. I was proud that I had ridden a bicycle for such a long distance. If I had been in a car I doubt I would have had nearly as much fun or as many lessons about life.

My biggest lesson was that nothing is impossible. There have been many other brave souls who have attempted or achieved feats much more difficult than this. You can do anything you want if you are determined enough. The only thing that holds you back in life is you.

MOUNTAIN SQUIRREL

MOUNTAIN BEAR

MOUNTAIN COW

MOUNTAIN???

YOU CAN DO ANYTHING

YOU DESERVE THE BEST

What are your dreams? Where do you want to go, what do you want to be, who do you want to be friends with? Follow your heart and your intuition. Your existence here is not about what you should do, or what you have to do, or what your dad thinks, or your religion thinks. It's about you.

Appreciate the simple little things. Be happy with whatever you have, wherever you are. I can guarantee you that there is some-one else who has it tougher than you.

You just never know what the Universe has in store for you. Learn to let things happen in your life instead of trying to make everything happen. So much of Western society is based on get-ting it all, but it ALL comes one step at a time.

I also realized that there are loving, generous people on every sin-gle corner of Planet Earth. Can you imagine what the world would be like if there were only happy, loving people? Let's focus on what's right in our society.

It was thousands of people, giving whatever they could, that made this trip a reality. I got everything I had hoped for and more. Whether it was with a meal, money, or by sending us happy thoughts, thank you to all those happy spirits who helped us on our way. Thanks to the big guy in the sky, thanks to Gramma Schredd, and thank you for reading my book and letting me share a little bit of Ted with you.

ALMOST THE END

Read
all this stuff
after you have read
the other stuff

EnviroRide was really the beginning. Exactly five weeks after I returned I was hired for a radio job with Z-95.3 FM. Brad, the program director for Z-95, liked my crazy idea for the morning show. For two years I worked at the most listened to FM radio station in western Canada as "Vancouver's Only Traffic Reporter on a Bicycle." Maybe the only one in the world. For three hours every morning, Monday through Friday, I rode my bicycle and gave reports on the morning commute. Even though I thought radio was my dream career, the trip and the radio job helped to uncover an even deeper dream, writing books. I had never considered writing or cartooning before the bike ride. Now there's this book.

Deanna works as an intensive care nurse. She learned to ski, snowboard, rollerblade, and juggle and is willing to try just about anything! We live in East Vancouver and have a huge vegetable garden. Dee and I are more in love than we have ever been before. One weekend last summer as we sat around our fire during a camping trip we decided to explore how we felt about our marriage. We both looked back to the best moments we have had together and realized that our most invigorating experiences were on the bike trip.

So in order to increase our "invigoration" levels we decided we should hit the highway again. In the summer of '96 Ted and Dee are departing on a Round-the-World Bicycle Tour in search of who has the most fun. We expect it to take somewhere between two and four years. Basically we want to travel on our bicycles wherever the wind blows us. I promise to keep you posted!

Give with love to whomever is placed in your path,
and let the superstar shine in your life.
I love you, I love you.

Ted Schredd

Lean on me

The following people have either inspired me, helped me out, or have just been good people above and beyond the call of duty. Thanks to everyone! See if you can find somebody you know on the list. There is a prize if you know more than fifty-two people on the list.

Our Stuffed Animals: Tookie, Schmama, Roog Doog, and Rick the Cow.

From the Land of the Big Mall: Dave Loosely, Mark Mishio, Mel Campbell and family, Rick Klinger, Brian Klinger, Mylar Hodson, Scott Parnwell, Al Ha Ha Ha Harris, Cam "Bang-a-bass" Beech, Anthony Greenham (what perm?), Chris Gargus, Enzo Corbo, Billy Varvus, Lisa Zimmer, Mike Nousek, Candace Hogan, Zoltan and Zig Dudas, Reg McNee, Colin Tkachuk, Ross Katona, Dean & Brenda Pohranychny, Darren and Randy Platt, Larry & Becky Wilkins, Terry Wilkins, Rod & Hali Foster, Les & Lori Petraschuk, Roooly Bigelow, Laurie Smith, Danny & Dena Buck, Hamie Donaldson, Kemp (I hope you're still with us), Rich Skelly, Todd Peever, Dale Sorochan, Robin Park, Scott Fraser, Sean Paustian, Terry Huculak, Angela Feist, Troy Ranger, and Brad Bischota.

Lake Louise: Rockin' Bob Tricky Turner Richenberger & Maude, Laurie Flahr, Tim Sless, Kelly Strutt, Ken Avis, Lynn and Donna Mae Wilson, Murray Drummond, Dave Toews, Scott Cumming, Sarah Sloane, J.J., Lee Benoit (Where the hell are you?), Leah Springman, Pete Herringer, Sean Lilly, Dave Craig, Rebecca Pollard, Rachel Chantler, Mickey, Bent, Deli Dean, Mark Riegert, Tony Kuijt, Pam Finch, Conrad & Rachelle.

Dogs: Betty, Biff, Buddy, Bobs, Boy, Brit, Willy, Wally, Damien, Sal, Stella, Clyde, Sam, Schatzi, Connie & Howard.

Vancouver: Dan Funk, Cindy Nickel, Chris Carter from Seymour, Adam Bersen, Mike Kaweski, Maria Filyk, Dave "Dr. Damage" Clements, Rob Wallace, Casey Cruz, Heather Johnston, Laurie Thompson, Brian Hill, Mike Playfair, Joe Playfair, Grant Lowndes,

Doug Grant, Kat Stewart, Bill Verchere, Craig Campbell, Howie & Dot, Cynthia Carlisli, Chris Hewart, Scott Fullmer, John Martin, Wayne Maxwell, Bob and Beverly Switzer, Tam Deachman.

Just some of the thousands of people that helped out EnviroRide: Rock, Paper, Scissors; Davey Jones, Toby Berner, Scott Owen, Doug Funk, The Coast Hotel, Koala Springs, Craig Stewart, Mike Raffan, Ski Optiks, The Comfort Inn, Allen Schinkel, Wayne & Todd from Alley Cat Bike Rentals, Sandy Beach (alias Sandy Ven Den Ham), Cathy Charabin, Bob Beaver, Thomas Hemmy, Marilyn Waller, Charonne Sinclaire, Terry Kreitz, Geo Purdie and Andrew Rogers, Ann Gill-Lawson, Susan McDonald, Mary McTier, Bill Suttles, John Fogerty & family, Bill and Moira from Chicago, Steve Lyman, Rob Krug, Rob "Milk it for all it's worth" Daniels, Grouse Mountain, Seymour Mountain, Rob (I have a porsche and a condo in Whistler and I'm not even thirty) Gietl from Dominoes Pizza, Okanagan Cider, Keg Caesars, John Fogerty and family, Tammi and Acea, Farmer Bob, Lisa & Graham, Joe & Holly, Carolyn Wright, Virgil and Carol Schmidt, Jil & Paul, Andrew the Aussie, KIMYA House, Bill, Connie, and Adam Chapman, Jose Luis, Andy Telfer, Ron & Nashoma, Barbara & Michael Melman, Jacques Eppich, Larry Laird, Duke Dixon, Poova & Lu at the Arena Hotel in San Jose, James & Jeanne Rasmussen, Carol White the friendly security gaurd, Arnie & Denise Placencio, Nadia Frankel, Amy Berard from Wham-O and her husband Steve, Jonathan Hulsh, Matt & Kelly, Charles (can I give some money to bikers) Jessey, Al Nolan from Nolan's Camera in La Jolla, Jan Seligman, Lou and Dorothy Sherbank, Julie Iriondo, Milton and Jean Phillips, Anja Hedtfield, Ken & Betty Preuit, Phil Smith in Tucson, Aleck MacKinnon for taking the great cover photo and his lovely fiancée Vivian, John & Melissa, Priscilla Colunga & Julian & Mama & Papa in Fredericksburg, ETO-WI-SET or Riley who did the magic on the bike, Aurielo Martinez, Richard Joseph, Will (Here's two dollars) Donald, Erin Nielsen, Lorraine Lockett, Simon Coutts of Simon's Cycle Shop, Andrew Hunter, Stanley Park Boat Rentals, Za's Pizza, KC & Randa Weiner, Patrick Burke, Lewis, Luther, and Maime Stoute, Murphy at the Gulf Hotel in Gulf Breezes, The Breaux family, Bill and Patsy Michaels, Mary and all the staff at The Dutchover Restaurant in Balmorrhea, Sandylee Toddy, Pistol Pete, Kim Golden, Rachel Kadansky, James (Sweat Pea) Morton, Matthew Bible, Linda Adams, Carl and Diane Hunter, Wilton Comardelle, Rudy Lee, Mary and David Lucas, Edwin & Lulu Perry, Curtis & Doris Gwaltney, Reverend Daniel Harvey, LANI MALLORY, LANI MALLORY, LANI MALLORY, LANI MALLORY (she likes it when her name is mentioned a lot), Pat Share and the rest of the staff at the Key West Holiday Inn, Mike and Jan from the Surfside Fire Department, Keith Rogers for letting us pig out in his buffet at the KFC in Southport, NC, Liz Wood & Dawn Perry, Brian Alleva, Dr. Ren Halverson, Bruce and Sharon at K-97 Edmonton, all the staff at Z-100 in Portland but especially Tony Martinez for still talking to me after Lisa went home, our friend the Universe, Estelle at KMUD in Garberville, David "Scooter" and the squatting bride Beth, Mike George at the Ogden Fire Department, Jim Gant, Cody & Edward at the Awendaw Fire Dept. #7, LANI MALLORY, LANI MALLORY, LANI MALLORY, LANI MALLORY, Tanya Arrogante and Mary from the Davis Corner Volunteer Rescue Squad, Billy and Fred Iapalucci for letting Dee get on the tractor and drive!, Shelby and Paul Spoon, Kal &

Carole, Lynn Cheffins and her eight dogs: Ernie, Rodney, Queenie, Tally, Kinnee, Prairie, Tanner, Phantom; T.C. Pipkin, Larry Pritchard & Joan, Bruce Cohen from Dana Point Cycles (for begging for bread from the bakery next door), Tin O'Hagen at Bike and Hike in Santa Barbara, Martin Hansen at The Sunshine Bicycle Center in Petaluma, David and Doris Sturgeon, Second Nature Bicycles in Eugene, Janet and Nishi at Foothills Cyclery in San Luis Obispo, Gloria (cook you a meal that will make your palate turn to rainbows) Gibb, Rick (have a hundred bucks) Cameron, Arnie Holmes, Forest & Mary Speaks, Eric Douglas in Albany for giving us *Leaves of Grass*, Tooker Gomberg the cycling politician, LANI MALLORY, LANI MALLORY, LANI MALLORY, LANI MALLORY, Rob Bryce of Scotland, Patty Dick at the Van Damme State Park, Eric Douglas, Bill and Roseanne, Howard "Turbo" Steed, Mike Eden at the Eden House Motel in Key West Florida, Bill, Matt, and Julie in Tampa, Kate Stadig & Chris, Mark Tomacci, Shelley & Klaus Moelleil for sending us beautiful rings to exchange for food, Monica Sepulveda the psychic that said we would make it, Amy Schoneman and family, David Kepron & Lou Hanessian, Mark Realini, Mike and Sheila Langenfeld of Illinois, Bryon Pierce, Johnny the wrestler, Pat and Scott (the four cool fireguys), Kansas (not the state just the person), Abundio Montejano, Gary Doud of Illinois, Eric Weber, Karen Drinkwater, Rogerio Araujo, Gilbert Youmans, Kurt Goff and his love affair with C.H., Kevin Connor & Cecilia Nasty at KGSR, Stephen Feig, Lori Ann Monsewicz, Christina Younger (Future Barbara Walters), Rob By at the "Liz," Steve Southwick KSNI, Ben Hayes KUHL, Gary and Lorraine Schiavi, Cori at KTZN, Mark Steven and Marianne Dupree at KMBY, Stephanie at KOME, Doc on KROQ, Dan Nimms at KUGN, Ed Severson, Wes Elliott, John Fogerty, Steve Brown at 97 Magic FM, Kim Golden, K.C. and Lisa, Carl Ream, Mark Spence, and CBC Montreal. Z-95: Martin Cassels, Lloyd Stoneman, Jeff Leroux, Andrea Ring, Matt McBride, Les Nielsen, Brad Phillips, Brad Edwards, Mark "Big Daddy" Hoadley, Jack Simmons, Jo-Jo Nickolls, Craig Chambers & Mike Bowman (for getting in trouble at the staff picnic for throwing big rocks at a passing train), Red Robinson (my broadcasting hero), Darren Parkman, Joanna Mileos, Steve Bush, David Hawkes, Kim Wooder, Mary Chang, Claudine Grant, Carol Carter, Carolyn Campbell, Mari-Lou Shoulak, Rick Holmes, Al Ferraby, Dannie Thiel, Victoria and her ultra cool husband; Ed, Tracey "Spork" Mills, Tamara Taggart, Valerie Burgess the greatest receptionist in the world, Susan Smith, Debbie & Coco, Clay St. Thomas, and Janice Ungaro, and all the other staff. A big thank you to all the fans who listened to me on Z-95 FM. Mike McCardell of BCTV and Marke Driesschen of CKVU, Carrie Brown from the *Georgia Straight*, Jamie Pitblado and Sharon Chan from the *Province*, Evelyn Gut and Toni Dawson of the Plaza 500 for making breakfast for me and my bike, Julie Prescott, Cycling B.C., Paul Jeffrey and his unbelievable hospitality in the most beautiful hotel ever, The Empress in Victoria, BC, Mark Hope, Astrid Cameron from Powerbar, Rob Jennings and Carey Wong from Alpine Promotions, Nancy Chilton, Sydney Cameron, Paul Bogaert from The Bike 'n' Board Doctor, Kevin Thomson from Carpe Diem, Paul Wiebe from Norco, Sean at Rollerblade, Victor Gautreau from Asama Bicycles, Blair Ivans from Subway, Steve Rough at Waterski World, David and Carol from Sugoi, Holly Kemp at Recreation Rentals, Ben Razavi, Allan Shiveral, Charmaine Crooks, Dennis Clarke from A&B Sound, Gord Inglis, Jayne Akizuki of the Cycle Show, Constable Cal Traversy &

Constable Tony Chambers (Cops), Janine Carpino from Bugaboos, Dave and Mark from Environment Canada.

Back in Vancouver: The five beautiful Australian Princesses—Naomi Millie, Kellie Yandle, Maureen Sullivan, Stacey Patterson, Kyle Beauliv who always bakes cookies for us when we go camping, Kurt & Lisa Hoppe, the Kiwi; Karl North, Harreson Martel, Steve Drew, Kitt Gleason, Jacque Blackstone, Mark Halliday the snowboarder extraordinare, Scott (extra-niffy-biffo-keen) Milne the world's greatest footbag player, Shane Bonneau, Ted, Sabrina and the lovely Amber, Captain Bruce Palynchuk and his good friend Russell, Her majesty Wendy Palynchuk the "Queen of Fucking Everything," Donna Mayer, Andrea Felicella, Freddie and the Sandblasters, Chard Cook who can juggle with his feet, Tanis and her three-legged animal circus, Kyle Lumsden and Jeff Small "The Potato Kings," Colin Jarvis & Sonja, Tina Baird also known as Special Agent Tina, Hugh "Don't wanna grow up" McClelland, David Solomon, Andrea Baird tamer of wild exotic animals, Randy (pronounced rrrrrrRRandy) Hood and Valerie Guthrie, Jeff (I never help anybody move) Kletter, Joe "The Chief" Abbinante, Frank "The Bigger Chief" Abbinante, Paulo Mattorolo, Yvonne the Cantel Queen, Pavel (Big boots and big boobs) Pleskot, Keith Maynard, Mike and Debbie Harris, Sean Elwood, Michael "Oolwah" Blake, Sandi and Owen Wright (The sheep magic workers), Terry and Leanne Conrad, Roger Dean, Nicole Cummings, Trevor Neufeld, Carla Hansen, Doug Blessin, Sabrina Wilson, Adanan Hussein, Abbas Sadeghzadeh, Stephanie McNulty, Amar Sidhu, Denny Arsene because he gave us jobs, Andrew Slater, James & Tina, Stuart Wilde, Lynne Mutrie, all the Hunsburgers—Bryan, Codi, Kristin, Dylan, Mike and Karen. From CFMI: Samantha Ferris and Andy Frost for flipping tunes on the airwaves as I worked on through the night, Larry & Willy of CFOX, Geoff "see you at the next ski schmooz" Palmer, Erin Davis (did the very first radio interview for EnviroRide), Stu Jeffries, Jack Marion, Terry Reed, Marianne Jaromi, Jacqui Underwood, Dean Haglund, Steve and Tifany, Del Monte International, Earl Bob, Allan Hollender, Stephanie McNulty, Snakeboarding Kim, "Bust Loose" Bruce Wilson, Tracey Bell, Craig Marsden and the exciting Kramer, Andrea Thiessen, Johnny Desantis, Torrin Skjold-Pettersen, Leoni Corra who stole Deanna's bathing suit then tried to break in to our hotel room in Mazatlan at four in the morning wearing only the flowered pattern of Dee's bikini, Nick Battocletti and Nick Majkovic.

Book: I couldn't have dreamed of a more perfect editor than Carolyn Bateman, Stuart Deachman and his computer magic, Levente, Daniel Wood, Rose Cowles and her artisitic excellence, Paul Grescoe, Kirsten Fraser, Kristina Finley who took care of my journals, and Kevin Mutch.

Sesame Street: Carm and Adelle, Lisa and Piero, Bruno & Gulia, Sister Anna Maria Bilotta, Sister Margaret Mary Schissler, Sister Beth Ann Dillon, even though they may not approve of the cover of the book or some of the things I say, these sisters are true gems, Mike the pizza guy from Dijo's, Dave from the Video store, Vinnie from the other Video store, Nick the Mailman, Santino Santoro, Bill my main haircut man, all the great staff at Safeway including Laura Lippucci, Kris Poirier, June Tarling, Gerry "the happy guy" Aneroth, Amanda, Cathy, Mary, Glenn, but especially Diane Hamada who chased me around the store with a free donut every time I went there, Noor and Rahem Rahemtulla, my dentist Art "Pain" Shippam, and his assistants Marilyn, Maureen, and Lisa, and of course the businessman of the nineties Phil at Kitzco in Downtown Vancouver, please spend all your money there so Phil won't be bitchy.

Svenland: Michael Brandt-Lassen from Denmark, also known as "Sven." You may have heard of him: he is very famous for his big smile and excellent jokes.

Family: my Mom and Dad, my sister Helen and brother-in-law Brian, brothers—Edward, Jim, Tom, Chuck. Plus Bobbie and baby Eddie, Auntie Marion and Uncle Connie, George and Heidi, Alex, and Peter, Gramma, and Auntie Clarice.

The Love Zone: Ted Loo, Larry Hope, Debra Edwards, Patrick Houser, Clarita Riccobono, Agnes Cookson, Tom Sofka, Kathy Steer, Kathleen Obley, Beth, Barry, and Brandon Leafman, Sonya Tomaszewski, Beverly and Logan (the spectacular ones), Hans Ter Horst, Allison Gillespie, Julie Harris, Merri Thornton, Bonnie Bradshaw, Jerry and Pattie Marshall, Annette Melmon, Paul Flashner, Zoe Ferguson (soon to be the first female President of the United States), Sage Ferguson, Martha Adams, Peggy Heber, Shane Madden, Cedar and Willow Mannen, Leslie Moor, Will Noyes, Kent Richards, Ayesha Star and Joy Star, Mikal the drug-crazed cook from Kauai, Zak, Brother "A" for Alapai, Cori & Doug, Tracey Tager, Avonlie Wilson, Alan Jacques, and all the other light warriors on the planet!

Dee's World: Jan & Nick Burns, Stephanie Brezina, Mim & Jeff, Cleo Bell, Mike Koppel, Michael Koppel and Michelle, Autumn and Jessica, Eddie Freeman, Lisa Williams, Judy & Bob, and Dee's kitties; Lucy and Orange Blossom.

You know how sometimes you won't think about a person for years then all of a sudden this warm memory comes back to flood your mental theater. Well, I had many warm memories writing this list, but I know there are still a couple more memories that will pop out of my head a year from now. So if for some reason your name is not here, either I haven't met you yet or the warm memory is in storage right now. I hope that you will remember to acknowledge the people who support you because without them, who's going to support you?